Living in God's Rest

At Peace in a Chaotic World

Nancy LaPointe

WestBow
PRESS
A DIVISION OF THOMAS NELSON

WestBow Press books may be ordered through booksellers or by contacting:

WestBow Press
A Division of Thomas Nelson
1663 Liberty Drive
Bloomington, IN 47403
www.westbowpress.com
1-(866) 928-1240

ISBN: 978-1-4497-8123-1 (sc)
ISBN: 978-1-4497-8124-8 (e)

Library of Congress Control Number: 2012924358

Printed in the United States of America

WestBow Press rev. date: 1/4/2013

To my Lord and Savior Jesus Christ, who continues to teach me hourly how to live in His rest.

Table of Contents

Acknowledgements...ix

Introduction...xi

Chapter 1   What is 'God's Rest' and
             Why do we need it?..........................1

Chapter 2   Chaos Abounds...............................9

Chapter 3   The times in which we live 17

Chapter 4   So many aspects of resting.............23

Chapter 5   Running To and Fro 35

Chapter 6   Faith and Trust 45

Chapter 7   Renewing your mind......................59

Chapter 8   Our Identity in Christ...................69

Chapter 9   Spiritual Roots of Physical Distress79

Chapter 10   Damaged Emotions
             and God's Rest...............................87

Chapter 11   What does change look like? 103

Chapter 12   What about the devil? 111

Chapter 13   The Sovereignty of God 119

Chapter 14   Suffering and God's Rest 131

Chapter 15   Hebrews 4: Sabbath Rest 139

Chapter 16   Is it Well with My Soul? 147

Appendix A 159

Appendix B 161

Acknowledgements

It is with heartfelt gratitude that I thank the following people for their ongoing love and support as I took the big risk of writing this book:

My husband Hank, the comma cop, who models unconditional love and allows me to spread my wings;

My daughter Carla and granddaughter Samantha, my computer gurus, who bring so much joy to my days;

My parents Bud and Olga Harkey, my sisters Sandy Dimsha and Teri Turner, and my brother Alan Harkey and their spouses and kids--- a family who is always loving and supportive in all that I attempt to do;

My inspirational writer friend Sandi Browne, who

instructs me and spurs me on when I want to quit writing;

The wonderful people at West Bow Press who made this first endeavor a smooth and enjoyable adventure;

So many other friends and family members who believe in me and love me no matter what crazy ideas I come up with. Wish I could name you all, but you know who you are.

You all are what makes life good. I love you.

Introduction

God's mercies are new every morning. For two long years, my husband and I depended on God's mercies hourly. After the state legislature dissolved the position I had held for four years, his retirement income was insufficient to cover our living expenses. An army veteran who contracted multiple disabilities from Agent Orange, an herbicide used during the Vietnam war, he had applied for total disability. The Veteran's Administration does not do anything quickly. Waking to the daily question of how to handle mounting bills and precarious health issues, some days we felt as though we were hanging on by a thread. We prayed, we claimed scriptures, we spoke positive affirmations, we encouraged each other. Each day brought new challenges from home repair needs to medical crises. Waiting became our nemesis. Six months into our waiting game, he was diagnosed with a melanoma, requiring surgery and more waiting. Waiting for a determination regarding whether it was benign or malignant; whether it had spread or not. Meanwhile, bills were rolling in. We dealt with aging parents and finally, the loss of my father-in-law. We were forced to place my mother-in-law in an Alzheimer's facility because we could not care for her. Our adult children had issues that needed our assistance. Hour by hour, day by day, we waited. We waited for the VA disability decision; we waited for a new job for me; we waited for God to deliver us from constant challenges that seemed out of our control. And God told me to "rest."

As God was teaching me innumerable lessons on the subject of His rest, I could not keep them to myself. I shared these revelations with friends and after much prayer, felt that one reason for these lessons was to share them with others.

When God began impressing me to "rest", I had been working long hours and pushing myself hard. I took it to mean physical rest. Since He told me to do it, I shed my guilt over taking naps or going to bed early or sleeping in late. Resting meant I could relax and enjoy a book or some good music, because if God told me to do it, I had to be obedient. But, the Lord had much more in mind; so much more.

Have you ever had God send you a message and no matter where you went or what you were reading or listening to, the same message just kept coming? This was one of those times for me. I found many scriptures about His rest and many applications to my life. He was and is serious about all of us "getting it."

I hope that you are reading this because He is leading you into a deeper understanding of what it means to enter His rest. I realize now that God has been teaching me how to live in His rest all my life. As I share some of my personal life experiences, my prayer is that they will encourage you in your journey as well.

> *Because of the Lord's great love, we are not consumed, for His compassions never fail. They are new every morning; great is your faithfulness. Lamentations 3:22-23*

Chapter 1

What is 'God's Rest' and Why do we need it?

"May your unfailing love rest upon us, O Lord, even as we put our hope in you. Psalm 33:22

It was late afternoon and the West Texas skies were filled with dust. I covered my baby's whole body with a blanket so she would not inhale the gritty dirt flying into our faces as we left the hospital. After all, this outing could be her last. I drove home with the doctor's words echoing in my head: "There's nothing more we can do. There's no need to keep her hospitalized any longer. Just keep a close watch on her and rest all you can." Rest. What parent could comprehend the meaning of that word when her only child was dying? After dozens of tests of every kind, my daughter had no diagnosis except "failure to thrive" and at eighteen months of age, was slowly starving to death because her body would not absorb the necessary nutrients for life. In essence, we were heading home to allow her to die in her own bedroom instead of a sterile medical environment. Rest? I daresay that rest was the last thing on my list. I'm certain that I did not rest in any sense, body, soul or spirit. I worried, I grieved, I was sick and I was angry. How does one rest in such a situation?

Resting is an interesting concept. If you were asked to draw a picture illustrating "rest" you might sketch a comfy chair, a hammock, or a person meditating or propping his feet up by a lake. It is a relaxed posture, a calm, quiet state. Most people would define rest in positive terms, believing it is a good thing. God spent six days creating the world, and on the seventh day He rested. Genesis 2 tells us that God finished His work, chose the seventh day to rest from that work and called that day of rest "holy." He valued rest enough to proclaim it to be holy.

We will see, as we explore resting in God, that His word contains many applications of "resting" and they are critical to living an abundant life. Resting is much more than taking a nap or stopping our frantic pace of life for a quick breather before running onward. The truth is that if you do not know how to rest in God, your attempts at attaining inner peace will prove futile. And, if you're like I was during stressful days, you've probably tried all types of ways to find that place of peaceful security and perhaps those attempts have not proven to have lasting value. Chasing after the world's ways with all its remedies and self-help books may offer some temporary relief, but in the long haul usually leaves us out in the cold. Entering God's rest elevates us to another level; to a deeper spiritual growth that requires some maturity, but reaps great rewards.

Resting on eagle's wings

Isaiah 40:31 says that He will lift us up on eagle's wings. Can you imagine yourself resting on an eagle's wing as he glides through space, floating over snow-capped mountain peaks and tall pine trees? Think about the sounds in the air above the flurry of the world, the quietness that an eagle soaks in as he soars above it all. Capture the essence of floating on air, relaxed in the breezes with those powerful wings securely carrying you wherever.

One element of entering God's rest is learning to

abide in the shelter of His wings, which means living so close to Him that we can hear His heartbeat. We have to learn to live there, because our human nature is to jump out of the nest and prove to the world how great we can fly on our own. That process is a good and healthy one, even necessary, but usually we run around in circles doing a whole lot of unnecessary busy work because we are proving that we can do it all ourselves. When we falter and crash, we may look for someone or something to blame, even God, but eventually we get up, dust off our wings and fly again. We have some clear, successful flights, which strengthen us to continue on our independent course. Then comes that day when we find ourselves nosediving into a cold, dirty lake. We crawl out, bruised and battered, and ask God why, why, why didn't He prevent that little detour. We then go into a self-pity mode, comparing our flight to other birds' and either get downright angry, which can go on for decades or into depression which again, can prolong the misery indefinitely.

We learn by trial and error how to navigate rocky waters or the clogged airspace of life and be strengthened to face the next trial. Those who can learn to grow through their crashes are the ones who are filled with character and wisdom. That wisdom that sustains and strengthens does not come from within ourselves alone, but blossoms through a partnership with God who is all wisdom.

Psalm 91 provides us with so many beautiful answers to questions we are usually too busy to ask. It reassures us that when we are dwelling in the shelter of God's plans, we are protected, shielded and cared for at a level most of us have not begun to comprehend. This is the hiding place mentioned in Psalm 91, a place of peace, and of rest.

He who dwells in the shelter of the Most High, will rest in the shadow of the Almighty. I will say of the Lord, "He is my refuge and my fortress, my God in whom I trust." Surely He will save you from the fowler's snare and from the deadly pestilence. He will cover you with his feathers, and under his wings you will find refuge; His faithfulness will be your shield and rampart. You will not fear the terror of night, nor the arrow that flies by day, nor the pestilence that stalks in the darkness, nor the plague that destroys at midday. A thousand may fall at your side, ten thousand at your right hand, but it will not come near you. You will only observe with your eyes and see the punishment of the wicked. If you make the Most High your dwelling---even the Lord, who is my refuge---then no harm will befall you, no disaster will come near your tent. For He will command his angels concerning you, to guard you in all your ways; they will lift you up in their hands, so that you will not strike your foot against a stone. You will tread upon the lion and the cobra; you will trample the great lion and the serpent. "Because He loves me," says the Lord, "I will rescue him; I will protect him, for he acknowledges my name. He will call upon me, and I will answer him. I will be with him in trouble, I will deliver him and honor him with long life will I satisfy him and show him my salvation." Psalm 91

I find that meditating on this Psalm quiets my soul and stops worry. It causes me to take a deep breath and exhale slowly, relaxing. It reminds me that He is in control and all I have to do is rest in His cocoon of shelter. If I soak in His love for me, all fear melts away. This is a principle that took me years to fully appreciate. I'm sure I'm still learning it.

At the time of my baby's illness, had I known all that I know today about God's rest, I believe I would have handled things differently. This is not to say that I would have had no worry or fear, for I am human, but I believe I could have trusted God in a way that brought peace to my soul, understanding that His plans and purposes are always good, regardless of how they appear at the time.

One morning after a particularly stressful night with the baby very sick, the phone rang and on the other end of the line was a sweet, young Japanese medical student. She excitedly told me that she had spent days researching my baby's symptoms and she wanted me to bring her back to the Texas Tech Health Sciences Center for a test for gluten intolerance. (This was quite rare in 1976). I admit that my emotions did not match hers, for we had endured countless tests to no avail. I was always full of hope, however, that God would answer my prayers and spare her little life, so of course, I took her in. The test was positive for Celiac Disease, and through a strict regimen of dietary controls, my daughter, so near death, began to come back to life.

God's mercies are new every morning and that morning was particularly special to me! It would be one of my first huge lessons in learning to rest in Him.

Chapter 2

Chaos Abounds

Do not be anxious about anything, but in everything by prayer and petition, with thanksgiving, present your requests to God. And the peace of God, which surpasses all understanding, will guard your hearts and your minds in Christ Jesus.
Philippians 4:7

2011 had the most devastating weather events the world had seen in years. There were weeks where people were in tornado shelters more than in their bedrooms. Schools were closed and businesses moved ahead at a snail's pace. One tornado after another claimed lives and ravaged structures. If you were a survivor of one of those storms, you could describe the stress better than I. Even those of us who were television observers can attest to the fact that upheaval at that level disrupts more than homes and businesses. In life's tragedies, insecurity attacks and becomes entrenched in people of every age and stage of life, as peace is stolen away in a brief moment of ferocious wind. But how many times have we listened to testimonies of survivors as they talk about coming out of the storm cellar to realize that nothing matters as much as faith, family and friends.

The survivors of Hurricane Katrina or the Japanese tsunami are examples of victors who press on when the odds are against them. These witnesses of the worst possible scenarios continue to testify of how their faith pulled them through and rekindled hope despite the mountains of rubble before them.

Pulitzer Prize-winning author Rick Bragg wrote: "As Southerners, we know that a man with a chain saw is worth 10 with a clipboard, that there is no hurt in this world, even in the storm of the century, that cannot be comforted with a casserole, and that faith, in the hereafter or in neighbors who help you through the here and now, cannot be knocked down."

A short time ago, June 8, 2012 to be exact, a horrible forest fire swept through the canyons surrounding our small community, burning over 200 structures, most of them homes, and many of them homes of my dear friends. Though warning calls were sent out for evacuation, many didn't receive a call, many were unable to salvage their precious belongings, and most was lost. Several were out of town so did not have a chance to protect or collect anything of value to them. We received a warning call, and then were ordered to evacuate our home around 1 a.m. Frantically making decisions about what to take and what to leave behind, we prayed over our home and rushed away with both vehicles and two dogs in tow. The sky over our home was glowing red as we watched bumper-to-bumper traffic wind its way down the mountain road leading to the main highway. Smoke was thick in the night air and the entire atmosphere had a surreal quality. My husband and I were fortunate to be able to drive to my Aunt Pat and Uncle Bob's home only a few miles out of the danger zone. For several nights, no one really slept. The days were long and filled with tension as we kept one ear on the local radio stations and our eyes fixed on the horrific looking skies. After six long days, we were able to return to our home, which had miraculously survived. Our hearts were broken, however, for our friends who had not been so blessed.

There are not words to describe the grief and the

anxiety that overcome those who survive sudden disasters. The aftermath prognosis remains to be written. Every survivor has a different story. The depth of each one's pain is at a level apart from the others. When a family loses their home and every worldly possession that was attached, it's easy to say that it's "just stuff." But, deep down inside, there is "stuff" that meant so much. Memorabilia, sentimental gifts, and family heirlooms gone. No matter how spiritually mature you are, it hurts.

Christians are quick to quote a scripture or righteous platitudes that we know are right, but the truth is the inner pain that stabs hearts in these times, does not connect adequately with those in the painful moments following a disaster. Does this mean that we lose our faith? Not at all. God created us to have emotions and in the time of tribulation we generally run the gamut.

Within the human psyche is a push, a pull, a will to win that takes charge and conquers. Adrenaline surges and inspiration abounds, and people rise to the challenges ahead. But what happens a few months later when the drudgery of cleaning up sets in; when the exhaustion takes hold from hours on hours of reorganizing and restoring. When government assistance has retreated, relatives have gone home, and bills are still showing up in the mailbox; that's when we need to understand what it means to enter God's rest. That's precisely the time we must run into the shelter of His wings, curl up against His heart, and rest.

Those dark nights when it seems too hard to carry on, those who dwell in the shelter of the Most High will rest in the shadow of the Almighty. (Psalm 91) Those who know how to rest in His shadow will truly rest. They will be in perfect peace. They will look at all the turmoil surrounding them, and say "You are my refuge, my fortress, my strong tower," and lie down and sleep in peaceful slumber.

If we really believe what we say we believe, as Christians, we have to look at the devastation surrounding us and then look up. We have to verbally and with our entire soul affirm that God is in control and that He is good and that whatever purpose He has in allowing disasters, we will be okay. We are grounded in the concepts we've studied in the Bible for years: that His ways are higher than our ways and most definitely better. His purposes have meaning that our daily priorities can't always comprehend or connect with. And we also know from past experiences that hindsight proves these purposes to be spot on; we learn and grow through our trials. What we want to be able to do, however, is to stop in the middle of the storm, no matter how horrible things appear, and say "it is well with my soul."

Maybe you don't believe that is possible. As we walk through this process of learning how to rest, step by step, you will begin to see that it is possible. If what you really want is the peace that surpasses all understanding, you can attain it. There are a few clouds to clear away, and a few concepts to unlearn from your past, but you can do it. You can be at peace in the worst of situations, if you learn to enter God's rest. This concept can literally change your life.

I firmly believe that many who have endured suffering and trauma over the past couple of years, such as my neighbors who lost all in the fires, are soldiers in training. Those people will openly share testimonies of all they have learned and how they have grown. God has trained them well, and those individuals will be the strong hands and feet of Jesus to others when they too undergo a disaster. The overcomers will be demonstrating to the world how to abide in God's rest. Their example and their inner peace will radiate a message of hope to an otherwise hopeless community. Most of all, they will exhibit how the ultimate joy in life is in knowing that God's priorities are all that really matter.

I lived for years in West Texas, specifically in an area known as "tornado alley." In the spring and in the fall, we were always on alert for watches and warnings. It was difficult to just relax and enjoy a rainstorm because we were constantly eyeing the cloud formations and getting prepared to take shelter.

My daughter shares that when she was small, she was tucked securely in her bed for the night, and inevitably would wake up in a makeshift bed constructed of a pile of blankets in the closet under the staircase. She never felt afraid. She knew it meant there were threatening storms and that I had carried her down and placed her in a safe spot until the storm had passed. She would just snuggle down deeply into the blankets and sleep peacefully.

To me, that's an excellent example of what our Father does for us. He carries us away from the danger of the storm, and tucks us securely into a safe place, His arms, and protects us until the storm passes over.

I lift up my eyes to the hills; where does my help come from? My help comes from the Lord, the Maker of heaven and earth. He will not let your foot slip; he who watches over you will not slumber; indeed, he who watches over Israel will neither slumber nor sleep. The Lord watches over you; the Lord is your shade at your right hand; the sun will not harm you by day, nor the moon by night. The Lord will keep you from all harm; he will watch over your life; the Lord will watch over your coming and going both now and forevermore. Psalm 121

Chapter 3

The times in which we live

"O God our savior.....who stills the roaring of the seas...and the turmoil of the nations." Psalm 65:5-7

You would have to be a total iconoclastic hermit to be living in this decade and not have some awareness of events taking place around us that are chaotic. The other night we were watching the news on television. There was a short video clip of some 'occupiers' who had gone way out of control, with violence, fires burning, police trying to contain it all and to the viewers it appeared to be a frightening and frenzied mess. We discussed how we have watched this kind of mayhem in other countries for years, but we never expected to be seeing it in our own country. It felt sad to realize that these days there is an increasing unrest, an escalating level of fear, violence, rebellion and evil all around us. Life will never go back to the times when we could let our children play ball in the neighborhood unsupervised or take a brisk walk in the nighttime air. We live in an unsafe world. Politics are corrupt, leaders disappoint us, and we sense a warning in the atmosphere that keeps us alert and prepared for even worse to come. Many of us have lost jobs because of budget cuts and are hearing threats of economic collapse on the horizon.

This is not a very encouraging scenario; however, you already know it's true. This is not a news flash that has stunned you. The reason I know that God has led me to write about entering His rest is because in the midst of severe stress and uncertainty, He has taught me how we can walk in perfect peace. You can watch the evening news, open your bank statement, answer that dreaded phone call from your child's teacher, or get betrayed by your best friend and still have the peace that surpasses all understanding. You can be living in "His rest" and be the healthiest, most peaceful, faith-filled person in town.

Taking a serious assessment of the state of our country, we can make an educated guess that in the days to come, we will be tested and tried. We will probably endure situations that we never thought we would have to endure, and we will be stretched beyond our comfort zone. The only way we will do well is to be living in His rest. I have been in training in this area for a while now, and have seen remarkable progress in my life. I know it is possible to walk in peace, trusting God and being secure. Security is a key to our emotional and spiritual well-being, and of course, it transfers to our physical health as well. The most important step for you to take at this point, is to believe that it is possible for you to let go of all fear, anxiety, worry and doubt. You must believe you can do it. If you don't, then go to God and tell Him how much you want to believe it and ask for His help. It will be the best request you ever make.

Years ago, I was involved with a man who was abusive. As with most of those situations, he didn't start out showing his true colors. After a stormy, painful time of heartbreaking abuse, I was able to get free of that relationship. But this man stalked me for almost a year. He made threatening phone calls, hovered across the street from my home and my parents' home, and made veiled threats to my friends. It was a very stressful time in my life. I had to keep my eyes on my rearview mirror everywhere I drove. I was obsessive about locking doors, overprotective of my child, and startled at every small noise in the night. I lived for months without opening my drapes and feared for not only my life, but the lives of those I loved.

Most certainly, I wish that I knew then all that I know now about resting in my Lord. I did not rest at any level. My spirit, soul and body were worn down and exhausted. I did not share what was going on with anyone except my family and a few key people because I did not want to involve anyone else in the threats or fear. One day I decided to share the situation with a small prayer group at my church. A member of the group left with me that day and as we walked to the car, she said, "This is not a battle for you to fight alone. The battle is the Lord's. We will pray and fast with you, trusting in God's protection and justice, and you will see victory." I was stunned, especially that people would fast over my issues. It meant so much to me. The group did indeed fast and pray often, until the problem was resolved. During that time, they taught me the principles of donning the whole armor of God (Ephesians 6:10-18), (see Appendix B) believing in His answers, and trusting in His protection.

I have acquaintances who will not venture out alone at night for any reason. Some are fearful of driving alone to a nearby city to shop. One friend has a paranoia of any strange people she sees just walking in her neighborhood. Although we must be "wise as serpents and gentle as doves," as the scripture instructs, it's a shame that we live in so much fear. We have to use wisdom in all things, but how much of the beauty and sheer enjoyment of life do we miss if we constantly shape our days around fear. I will discuss fear in more detail later on, but for now, stop and make a brief assessment of how often fear dictates your plans or activities. Without a doubt, this might be interfering with your ability to rest in God.

Perhaps you need to stop spending time listening to multiple news reports or focusing on the turmoil in the world. We need to be aware, but overload can definitely bring us down. One of my favorite scriptures is in Philippians 4:

> *Finally, brethren, whatsoever is true, whatsoever is noble, whatsoever is right, whatsoever is pure, whatsoever is lovely, whatsoever is admirable --- if anything is excellent or praiseworthy---think about such things.....And the God of peace will be with you.*

> *Philippians 4:8-9*

Wherever our mind chooses to wander, our emotions will follow. If we choose to concentrate on that eagle's wings and how it feels to be resting there, gliding through life, towering above the fray, we are much more likely to have God's peace than when we are imagining the worst.

When I was being stalked and threatened, what if I had prayed, then trusted God totally, and rested in Him? What a different picture would be painted of those days. Truthfully, I would have avoided physical ailments that followed, such as colitis, gastritis and migraines. I would not have passed a spirit of fear on to my family. There are undoubtedly many other aftereffects of my inability to enter His rest.

I hope that by sharing the lessons I've learned you might be able to examine your own methods of handling life's crises. I pray that God will open your spiritual eyes to see how He can free you and hold you in His rest.

In repentance and rest is your salvation, in quietness and trust is your strength. Isaiah 30:15

Chapter 4

So many aspects of resting

Drop Thy still dews of quietness,

Till all our strivings cease;

Take from our souls the strain and stress,

And let our offered lives confess

The beauty of Thy peace.

-John Greenleaf Whittier

Many scriptures talk about entering God's rest and resting 'in Him'. As He led me to study this in depth this past year, I learned that it goes far beyond any simple definition of my own.

Resting in Him is understanding fully a benefit of the finished work of what Christ did for you on the cross. It is called a finished work because when he died on the cross, that ended, for those who believe, all human effort to save ourselves. It is ceasing all efforts to obtain anything by works or deeds. Resting means giving up, letting go of all our fleshly, humanly efforts to gain God's favor or to gain man's praise or approval. It means you understand that only in Him can you accomplish anything. By faith only do we walk in that place of rest. Our human condition prohibits our ability to do this on our own.

Resting is totally about trust. Trust is the foundation, the core, so that no matter what the circumstances, no matter what we see around us, that trust -- that rest -- is enveloping every part of us, so that we walk in peace--perfect peace. Perfect trust in Him, the God of the Universe, who created the world and created you.

> *Isaiah 26:3 says "He will keep in perfect peace, him whose mind is stayed (steadfastly) on Him." The Amplified Bible translates it: "You will guard him and keep him in perfect and constant peace whose mind (both its inclination and its character) is stayed on You, because He*

commits himself to You, leans on You, and hopes confidently in You."

"Worry is a cycle of inefficient thoughts whirling around a center of fear."

Corrie Ten Boom

In essence, resting means there is NO worry, stress, anxiety, or despair whatsoever. Those cannot coexist in the same mind/soul with His Rest. When our mind is in "His Rest" mode, we cannot be shaken. We are abiding in complete trust and faith that He is in complete control and we are not, and this is not only okay with us, but it is wonderful! God is Sovereign, which means He is not only in control, but He has all wisdom and knowledge by which to govern. He decides and acts on our behalf, for our good and knows what we need at all times. Our purpose, our calling and our gifts (from Him) are all to be used for His glory. When we get that firmly established and close our eyes to what people want, demand or think, we are entering the gateway to that place of rest.

Other people have not been as much a problem for me as I have been a problem for myself. I have stressed and struggled within myself so many times over what

I need to be "doing". God wants me "being" not doing. Once my mind (soul) is at rest in Him, "being" who He's called me to be, the "doing" will follow in a calm and relaxed manner as He leads. Busyness, activity and striving to gain His favor, His blessings or His love is a futile and exhausting endeavor. God's grace (defined as undeserved favor), is already ours. If you have submitted your life to the Lord, you are living under His grace. It's yours and no one can take it from you.

Exhausting ourselves, trying to make things happen, even good things, is our vain attempt to be in control instead of submitting to His control in every situation. If we are walking in unbelief and lack of faith, not resting in Him and not trusting Him, our lives become unmanageable and filled with anxiety. That anxiety is a product of focusing on "self" and thinking that it all depends solely on me or another person or situation. Where does that leave God?

In his book "Forgotten God" Francis Chan writes: "Nowhere in scripture do I see a balanced life with a little bit of God added in as an ideal for us to emulate." That concept is an example of living as though I am the center of the universe, following my plan and then asking God to come along and bless me or do what I want. Then, when things don't go so well, I get upset with God, when I'm actually doing everything backwards, leading to more stress than ever. We tend to live like gerbils on a wheel, running in circles with our plans, emotions and ideas. We tire ourselves out physically, emotionally and spiritually.

Entering God's rest is a wonderful solution. It takes away the heavy burden of me being responsible for the world's problems. I already have a Savior; I don't have to try to be one—to myself or to anyone else.

His rest in me will produce a spirit that illuminates and exudes peace no matter what the situation. This will draw others to the Lord far more than all the good works in the world. Others should be asking me the reason for my hope, my joy, my peace, especially in the midst of any storm I am battling or the whole world in chaos. Are people asking you the reason for your hope and peace?

One day when I thought I was finished studying God's rest, the Lord led me once again to scriptures about it. I opened my Bible to Joshua 1:13, which says,

> *"The Lord your God is giving you rest. You are to help your brothers until the Lord gives them rest as He has done for you, until they receive what God has for them."*

My counseling clients were asking questions which plunged into the deep well of understanding 'how' to rest in God. It seemed that almost every phone conversation with friends or family was also moving into the realm of losing stress by trusting God's sovereignty. God appeared to be quite serious about getting this message out and wanting us to comprehend it at a deeper level. I realized that He was not finished with me either; constant issues were arising to test my understanding of this concept.

For years I had been in ministry, mostly counseling, but serving as an associate pastor of a large church placed me in several different types of ministry. In those years, God's grace was definitely on me. I was always seeking and He was graciously answering. It was a busy time, but also a rewarding and fulfilling time of my life. I had many friends, a full social life and much joy. God's favor was on me through no works of my own. I understood that fully.

Then, life changed. My husband retired and after much prayer we felt confident about leaving the city in which we had been serving. We moved to our new place, a beautiful mountain resort town and began settling in. I had no doubt that I would just take up where I left off, with God opening doors of ministry and using me wherever He chose to do.

What actually happened was a five year wilderness experience. For five long years I struggled with isolation, loneliness and very little from God. We tried several different churches and home groups but didn't feel that we fit anywhere. We would meet couples we enjoyed and were not able to build relationships. Time rolled along and I fought depression.

My natural tendency is to decide that God is disciplining me. I must have done something out of his will; maybe even moving out of the town where we were serving. I spent almost three years battling that one. He did give me peace in that area, however. I then jumped into different areas of ministry, joining groups and volunteering to do all kinds of things. Not only was I missing fellowship with other believers, I knew it was right to use my gifts to serve and I was not doing that. I served and worked, but those things fizzled out and so did I.

Day after day, and night after long night, I cried out to the Lord. Why, after a successful ministry experience for so many years would He be finished with me? I studied every facet of pride. I had repenting to do there and certainly did that for some time. My desire was to lay down all of my own ambitions and know without any doubt that I was walking in God's will.

His message to me to rest continued to surface from time to time. I didn't fully understand it.

I struggled with conflicts over different teachers I had followed, realizing that some of them were not pure in their teaching of scripture, leading many astray. That was a painful truth to walk out, getting rid of many books and tapes I had and focusing solely on the Bible itself. I went to counselors and pastors to seek answers and prayer. Continued silence.

My prayer life became one of begging and pleading with God. He was mostly silent, month after month. I called friends and prayer partners from my previous town, and they graciously prayed with me and for me over those long years. They also seemed to have little to offer in why I was so alone. I continued to receive the word "rest" from them on several occasions.

The home where I live has a magnificent view of mountains, towering pine trees and gorgeous valleys. I sit on my deck in the early mornings and late evenings and watch the hummingbirds, deer and elk and listen to all kinds of birds singing. To me there is not another place on earth more peaceful and beautiful. In fact, it is another answer to prayer, because for many years I prayed that God would someday let me live here, and He did.

So imagine the conflict in my soul, sitting on my deck, praying, looking out over God's incredible creation and having no peace. I longed for human companionship. I longed even more for that communion with God that I had experienced for so many years that seemed to be gone. There was no resting in God at this point. I was in much turmoil.

Into my sixth year of isolation, things began to change. I got involved in a new church, a new ladies Bible study and made a friend who inspired me. God did not directly speak anything profound to me, but He let me know the wilderness experience was ending. That does not mean that everything became perfect; it definitely did not. But I knew in my spirit that I had grown spiritually and was stronger.

The 'rest' messages began infiltrating all facets of my life around this time. As I studied and prayed, I realized that I had depended far too strongly on people in my life. Dependence on God has to be the top priority. People come later. People are important and He created us to need each other. If we need people in order to walk in joy and peace, we are off track. I learned infinitely more through my wilderness trek, but that particular lesson was critical to my walk with God, as well as my ministry to others. Resting in Him means that if He chooses to isolate me from

31

all living beings, I can still be at peace and walk in joy each day.

I also learned that God leads people quite often into wilderness experiences. These times are appointed for a specific purpose. We can't always see the purpose at the outset. Our vision is like peering into a fogged over mirror. We see that God is still there, but we can't quite comprehend what it is He is out to accomplish in us. It requires time, energy, meditation and prayer to begin unfogging things. When the purposes begin to take form, it is an exciting time because we are reaffirmed. We are inspired, waking up to the realizations that God is unfolding and looking at our life in new and more focused ways. It reminds me of waking up in the morning groggy and slowly stretching and getting more and more alert to the environment surrounding me and then suddenly remembering it's my birthday. Only truthfully, God's epiphanies are far beyond that!

Wilderness experiences provide the perfect time to rest in God; however, after reading about several other people's times in the wilderness, I think it's pretty rare that people actually rest. It seems to be a time of wrestling with God, but at the end of the season, the rest comes more naturally. Lessons learned, new inspiration growing, and stronger trust abound.

Trust in the Lord with all your heart and lean not on your own understanding. In all your ways acknowledge Him and He will direct your paths.
Proverbs 3:5-6

Chapter 5

Running To and Fro

"...caught up in our own busyness, frantically running from one crisis to the next in a cycle that looks less like loving the Messiah and more like trying to become one." -Phileena Heuertz and Darren Prince

Our culture today thrives on activity. It is almost an idol. We have to be doing something every moment. We notice it most in our kids, constantly texting, playing games on their devices with earphones hanging out their ears, rocking to the beat. But adults are also in constant motion. Multitasking is an understatement. We are on our cell phones while driving, doing business while walking through the market and whipping out laptops or ipads even on an airplane flight for pleasure. I have noticed that I have trouble just sitting down to watch TV. I reach for my laptop and play solitaire while watching a movie. Why are we so restless? Our children are being treated for ADHD at alarming rates, and adults are now in that growing number as well. Studies on children between birth to 12 have shown that their brain activity is different from the brain activity of older people at that same age. They are beginning electronic activities at such an early age that their brains develop differently than those of us who grew up without electronics at our fingertips every moment. There are pros and cons to this phenomenon. Teachers have to teach differently and it spreads to all areas of life. Hyperactivity is an epidemic!

The American way is to focus on success, achievement, money, technology, and material wealth. We have become a society of greed and our hunger for things cannot be satiated. We feel we must have certain luxuries in our lives to be complete. The only problem is that no matter how much we get, we want more. We never feel complete because someone in front of us always has the dangling carrot of one more thing that we want to obtain. Even the humblest of Christians in this country is seen with the finest of material possessions. It is our way of life. We really don't know any other life. The poorest people in this country are rich in the eyes of those in third world countries. Yes, we do have poor in America. My point is that for most of you reading this right now, you know who you are, if you are honest, you know you have all you could ever need.

I was reading an interesting book by Michael Bunker, who asserts that electricity is at the root of all our problems. At first, I thought he was off-the-wall eccentric. But, as I read his justifications I saw the light (pardon the pun). As we look back throughout history, the early settlers who did not have electricity lived very simple lives. They worked hard, but their lives were basically simple. If you read stories of the most notable Christians who inspire us even now, they had a rich depth of insight which resulted from quiet times with God and family. (No, I do not want to give up my electricity! However, God just might have a different plan for us all.) Electricity, in the beginning, was lauded as a major source of providing time-saving innovations. Let me share an interesting excerpt from Bunker's book, Surviving Off Off-Grid:

> *"Saving time is not always "good". In fact, in very real terms, there is no such thing as saving time. Time may be reallocated, but never "saved". Some technologies promise to be "time-saving"*

> *when in reality none of us using that technology*
> *have any more time for spiritual pursuits than*
> *we had before the use of the technology. In fact,*
> *we quite often have less time, because we have to*
> *work to pay for and support the technology."*

The more toys we acquire, the more hours we must work to pay for them. The more toys we acquire, the more hours we spend playing with them. We have lost so much! We have lost precious time with family and friends and more importantly, we have lost precious time with our God. Our priorities are so out of order and the saddest thing about that is that we are too busy to realize it!

I would venture a guess that many people would not be attracted to a book about "rest" because the concept is foreign, and it's not a how-to book on making money or producing more of something. Those are the big sellers (on ebooks of course). Can you not see how this must grieve the heart of God? He tells us to "be still, and know that I am God." We have no clue how to be still. Many people share with me that they have never heard God speak to them. I see their lives, filled to the brim with active electronics never stopping the beeping and droiding, and I have no doubt that they are correct. God does not have to compete. Either He matters enough that we stop and listen to Him, or He does not.

Why is all this important to your ability to enter God's rest? The technology age has replaced the age of families sharing their stories, talking about their experiences and all they have learned over time. Now our kids just go to the internet for any answer to any question. Their parents probably aren't at home to ask the question, because they're working their tails off and if they are there, the kids won't ask because the kids don't want to take the time it would take away from getting to their games. A vicious cycle that leads to unhealthy relationships with family and with God. How many times do the children or the parents go to God to ask the questions? The internet is faster.

Not to belabor my point, but the societal norms we fall into become our gods. The busyness and striving to get more, do more, be more, is destroying who we were created to be. We have a veil over our eyes, only seeing what media presents as a successful, thriving person and it's all deception. In the midst of the chaos, we have days where we stop and ask God, "Why am I always so tired? Why can't I sleep? Why is my family such a mess? Why, why, why?" We give God about five minutes (maybe) and if we don't hear an answer, we then take some pills or whatever comfort is in the closet, and complain that God doesn't care. Then we go right back to our frenzied busyness.

I use electronics myself. I do not think that in and of themselves they are evil. I think it is an area where we need to stop and think --- without aids. Stop and process the Word of God and get quiet and still and see where He is leading. Hear what answers He has for us, because He definitely has them. He does not need any technological devices to solve problems or to provide answers for our life's difficult issues.

The most precious times I have experienced with God, when I heard Him speak truths to my spirit, were in times of quiet, uninterrupted space, waiting, meditating on His word and listening. Usually it does not happen quickly. I admit that at times that irritates me too. I want to run into my prayer room, pray for a few minutes, read a few scriptures, and then ask God a question and receive an instant answer. That has happened, but maybe only once or twice. God has a totally different idea. He desires fellowship with us, as His children, just as we long for sweet times of fellowship with our children. Times that are not about asking for anything; just loving and connecting at a higher level. Getting to know God is an empowering and exciting endeavor. Getting to know Him, just as getting to know another person in your life, takes intentional times of setting aside time, energy and desire to make it work. The busyness of your life must take a back seat and the glory of knowing God must become a priority.

If you are serious about having peace within yourself and living a more fruitful, peaceful life, you must make an honest assessment of how you are living and be willing to make some changes to your lifestyle. You will never regret it. God actually pushed me into this whole life change because I was serious in telling Him I wanted to be renewed and more fit for His service. He knew I meant it. It is not an easy process. I am still in the middle of it, I think. I do know that I have come miles and miles in a good direction. I see God and the world in a different light than I ever have, and have more peace in my soul.

"Do you sometimes wonder if our busyness — even for God — is often what's keeping us from being what God wants us to be?" ~ Kay Arthur

When the fire of prayer goes out, the barrenness of busyness takes over.

George Carey

The world is full of men and women who work too much, sleep too little, hardly ever exercise (or obsess over it), eat poorly and are always struggling or failing to find adequate time with their families. We are in a perpetual hurry-- constantly rushing from one activity to another, with little understanding of where all this activity is leading us. . . . The world has gone and got itself in an awful rush, to whose benefit I do not know. We are too busy for our own good. We need to slow down. Our lifestyles are destroying us. The worst part is, we are rushing east in search of a sunset. -Matthew Kelly

How do we transition from hyper to rest.....It's a huge jump! I happened on a website that might give you a smile as you contemplate making your changes.

International Institute of Not Doing Much IINDM

Slow Manifesto

There are those who urge us to speed. We resist!

We shall not flag or fail. We shall slow down in the office and on the roads. We shall slow down with growing confidence when all those around us are in a shrill state of hyperactivity (signifying nothing). We shall defend our state of calm, whatever the cost may be. We shall slow down in the fields and in the streets, we shall slow down in the hills, we shall never surrender!

> If you can slow down when all around you are speeding up, then you're one of us. Be proud that you are one of us and not one of them. For they are fast, and we are slow. If a thing is worth doing, it is worth doing slowly. Some are born to slowness—others have it thrust upon them. And still others know that lying in bed with a morning cup of tea is the supreme state for mankind.

How to Slow Down

Infectious multitasking is on the increase. If you're attempting to eat breakfast and floss at the same time, or if you take phone calls during your meditation practice, you could be in trouble. Are you trying to exercise and sleep simultaneously? These are the tell-tale signs of a debilitating medical condition known as gettingthingsdoneitis. Studies have shown that rushing is a direct cause of rudeness, blunder and mishap. Members of

IINDM understand all this and have embarked on the slow path to not much.

In all seriousness, however, if you are lacking the inner peace that is so critical to your well-being, please slow down, turn off the electronics, listen to your Father's voice and breathe deeply, knowing you are now on the right track.

Chapter 6

Faith and Trust

*Cast all your anxiety on him because
he cares for you. 1 Peter 5:7*

Lying on my back in a hospital bed one spring morning, I was tearfully looking at the ceiling and asking God why I had no peace. I was working two jobs, had a chronically ill child and numerous other ongoing issues. I may not have had any more problems than most women my age at that time, but I had poor coping skills. I was admitted to the hospital after collapsing at work. I was diagnosed with gastritis, colitis and migraines. I was a mess! My doctor strolled into my room that morning, pulled an extra chair backwards next to my bed, propped his cowboy boots up, and said "Well, Nance, don't ya think it's about time you decided to make some changes in your life?" I replied that I had no clue how to do that. He informed me that if I didn't make some changes -- and soon-- I was going to remain a very sick chick. My story following that episode is one for another day, but I went home, reevaluated my life and made some big changes. The biggest one was to begin to learn how to let go and let God be God. Worry and fear were eating me alive, literally.

Worry has no benefit to your physical health. It brings down your emotional health, and spiritually, well, it's a sin!! Sin takes root by infecting your mind, travels into your body and you end up a very unhealthy human. As Christians who are living with the Holy Spirit indwelling us, what is the meaning of the peace that surpasses all understanding? I can list over a hundred scriptures that instruct us to be not afraid; don't worry about anything; lay your burdens down; and on and on and on. Are those just for an encouraging devotional book on the shelf by your bed? Are they truth or are they not?

There are many rich, deep truths to absorb regarding entering God's rest. Our perception of living in His rest is directly related to the level of trust in which we live. Faith is believing what we cannot see and trust is much the same. At times we can see faith in action and at times we trust because we have already seen. Resting in God is having a belief, trust and faith that prevails over and prevents any trace of stress, fear or anxiety. It means we are walking in perfect peace. Again, that peace that surpasses all understanding.

At times life's events are swirling around me and I know that in my flesh I should be worrying. For some reason, I am calm, at peace. This has been a process that took many years to bring to completion. As I write this, I laugh, because I know it is not yet to completion, and won't be until I am standing on the holy ground of heaven, gazing at the face of my Jesus. However, my progress has been amazing! At one time of my life, worry could have been my middle name. In fact, I think that if I was not worrying, I was worried about why I was not worrying and that would lead to a whole new level of worrying. It seemed like if I was not worrying, it meant I didn't care. Or that I was not in control of my life. This makes no sense, but I know I am not alone in this belief system. We have so much erroneous thinking as we're developing through the years. Sometimes it comes from childhood experiences or traits passed down through generations. Those of us who have studied God's Word for years can quote so many scriptures to refute worry, but getting it from our head to our heart can take decades.

The scripture says *"it is for freedom that Christ has set us free."* (Romans 5:1) Think about that. Freedom. Do you live in freedom? Freedom means you are free. It means you are not chained, in bondage, drowning and suffocating. It means you breathe freely, relaxed, secure. It means you sleep soundly. You don't have nightmares or insomnia. It means you don't have migraines, muscle tension, stomach cramps, bad moods or temper tantrums. You are probably ready to tell me that those are part of normal life and dealing with the stresses the world brings. Yes, you're right, but only when you are not resting in your God. That is when you are trusting only in yourself or others.

If I were to ask you to explain what it means to you that Jesus was sacrificed, dying on a cross for you, what would you tell me? You would probably tell me that He died to save you from hell, that he died for your sins, and that because you believe in Him you get to spend eternity in heaven. That's a good answer. However, is there not a whole Bible full of scriptures teaching you what His finished work of dying on that cross and being resurrected from the dead does for your life now? Granted, our life on earth, in the grand scheme of things, is really just a small blip in time, but there are days that that blip feels to us like eternity.

I was watching Francis Chan on a video where he walked out on stage carrying a rope that trailed for a few hundred feet behind him. The handle, about 8 inches long, was white, and the remainder of the long rope was dark. He said the white portion represented our life on earth; the remainder our life in eternity. It was a very impressive visual example.

When we are dealing head-on with problems of jobs, children, spouses, finances and so on, life feels long. We have been bought with a price, a big price, and we need to live like it. We are co-heirs to the throne of God. The God of all time, of the whole universe, has gifted us with a capacity to live in freedom and that freedom is called His Rest. What do we do? We say "no, I choose to be chained to worry, stress and doubt." We don't say it aloud; we say it with our lifestyle.

Our lives are our testimony, our witness, of what we believe. If you live a stressed out, worried life, you probably have physical ailments that require medications and limit your life's activities. Our testimony to others is that we exist on medications because we are chained to the world and its value system which means there is no hope, no way out but this one. It means that we, as Christians, are not living any different life from non-believers, except that we are happy to know we are going to heaven when we die. For most of us, it is going to be awhile before we land in heaven. How are we living in the meantime?

You might decide while reading this that I just do not understand the difficult situations you are dealing with. You are right; I probably don't. Does that really matter? The real question is, do you believe God's word or not? Not long ago, I heard a teaching by Kay Arthur where she said the bottom line is that you either trust God--- or you don't. That's it. It struck a chord with me. Now I say it often. You either trust Him or you don't! It's really quite simple. If God is truth and His word is true and you believe in Him and you believe His word, your trust is strong and you live secure. Secure in His love, His protection, His provision and His omniscience, omnipotence, and omnipresence. He knows all, is all-powerful, and is everywhere you are at every moment. That's security! That's where rest enters the picture. Resting means peace (of body, soul and spirit) because we are secure at every level.

A couple of years ago, my job ended. I have worked

all of my adult life. I like to work. I was raised to have a strong work ethic. Not working, in my mind, has always been equated with laziness or having no ambition. As I mentioned in my introduction, the state legislature voted to suspend all funding for the program I was administering in my county. I have never had any trouble finding or keeping a job. I have a good education, good experience and good references. I have been happy to stand on that resume and believed that I would never be without work.

God had another idea for me. He decided that since my mouth is always saying how much I trust Him and how He is in control of all things, that He would just give me a little test. He is God and He has every right to do that. To me, it was not a little test. To me, it was a very big test; a monumental, mammoth-sized test! In our little community, there is not a plethora of job opportunities. That did not discourage me at all. I just trusted that God would give me the job I needed, as He always had before. I applied for every possible job that appeared online or in the papers, or by word of mouth. I prayed. I fasted. After a few weeks, turning into months when our savings began to dwindle, I started to stress. Not only was I not being offered any jobs, I was not even offered any interviews. During this time, my friends and family members were praying for me and several times someone would call and say that they felt God was saying for me to rest. Okay. I tried taking naps and sleeping more at night. I tried to practice all the de-stressing techniques I had taught my clients. I read God's word every day, often throughout the day and meditated on scriptures about worry, trust, faith and all those practical things.

Slowly, I became more stressed, more worried because I was beginning to see that it was easy to preach on faith and trust when your income was steady and adequate. When we reached a point where we had to decide whether to put some gas in the car or cut out the foods we liked, that was step one. Then, it moved on to paying the electric bill or getting shoes, when ours were worn out. It got steadily worse and we realized that pride was rearing its ugly head too. We couldn't join friends for dinner at a restaurant. We couldn't drive to a nearby town to check on my mother-in-law in an Alzheimer's facility. We couldn't buy gifts for family birthdays. It hurt.

Interestingly enough, every few days or weeks, God would once again send me a message about resting in Him. I got that message from morning email devotionals, TV preachers, friends on the phone, scripture after scripture, and radio talk show hosts as I was driving. Obviously, God wanted me to learn this one! I kept saying "Okay, God, I get it!" But, I'm sure He just smiled and nodded His head, saying, "sure you do." One day I had the realization that learning to live with very little money was like fasting from food. It brings to the surface all the ugly dross that is down inside you. Oh, I had been poor before when I was a young, single mom. I knew what it was like, but frankly, that was long ago and over the years I had remarried and worked hard and handled money well enough to never be without things that were important. There's a key word here too---"important." I was learning what was important and doing it the hard way.

One day I had a big epiphany. *God* was the reason I never got a job interview. He did not want me to have a job. My husband is retired and a disabled veteran, but has a fixed monthly income that was not enough to support the lifestyle to which we had become accustomed. (I suppose he also learned many lessons through this time of resting in God.) Days later, I heard the Holy Spirit speak to me that I did not need a job.

After a year and a half of struggling, more and more each month of course, some miracles occurred. One was that I gained a new appreciation of God's sovereignty. This was not lip service. He really was in control. I had no say in the matter. (Confession: occasionally, I would still check the job listings, knowing in my spirit it was not wise. Usually this was directly following a conversation with a well-meaning person who would be asking why I wasn't out beating the streets when we had no gas in the car.) Another blessing was that I saw my pride and went after that, repenting of my love for material things, and for thinking I could provide well.

All the time these lessons were being walked out, I was still getting the "rest" messages and studying it more and more. I slowly began to understand it deep in my spirit. Resting meant waking in the morning at peace and lying down at night in peace, not worrying about anything, in spite of my circumstances. A big miracle was that all our bills were continually paid and up to date. Some days my husband would be scratching his head and telling me there is no way this could be working. On paper, it was impossible. But God is our Provider!! He sent me counseling clients. He had certain people send us money at strategic times. At first I would argue and try to return the checks and the givers would say God told them to send it and that if I sent it back I would be robbing them of their own blessing as well as mine. (That pride thing in me again.)

One morning I was praying and God showed me that I had turned a corner. The biggest miracle of all had occurred. I was totally at peace. I was not worried. I was not stressed. And that particular day, we had $25 in the bank and a number of bills were due within the week. My husband had a little more angst at that time, but he was coming along quite nicely in the process too. I was just praising God and enjoying sitting in the sunshine looking out at the glorious pine trees and listening to the birds singing. And experiencing no guilt. This is what God's rest is all about. Knowing without any doubt that He is our Provider; that He is our Source, our Protector and our Peace. Entering His rest is wonderful! It takes all the world's remedies, medications, therapies and opinions and just tosses them over the cliff! Actually, this is what God's Word teaches us over and over again; we just don't quite get it. I have no doubt that some reading this would be very skeptical indeed. I would have as well, a few months ago. I would have said that person was not living in the real world.

Let's think about that phrase: living in the real world. The real world says that we must stay so busy that we live in a state of avoidance. Because if we face the truth of each day, we would be overwhelmed by it. Overwhelmed is not the state we want to live in if we are a child of God. Panicked, stressed and anxiety-ridden does not seem to fit the verse that says "the truth shall set you free." (John 8:32)

What are all these scriptures if not truth and if not intended to give us a better life? We sing the songs and teach our kids the Bible verses. Then, our kids watch us take anti-depressants, anti-anxiety tablets, and anti-whatever else medications so that we can keep on keepin' on. Something is wrong with this picture!

How can we profess to believe His Word and then live in a totally different realm?

This is not to put guilt on you if you take medications. It is meant to hopefully cause you to re-evaluate your lifestyle and thinking. Stinkin' thinkin' can be healed! There is a time for medications, but there is also a time for surrendering all to God and letting Him heal. Don't think that I am saying you are condemned for taking medications. I am not saying that at all! Some people need them and don't ever stop them without your doctor's approval. Stay tuned in to what I am trying to explain: there is a path to healing that can take you off those meds and bring you into a better way of life.

There is a pathway to change. It is possible to be transformed, by the renewing of your mind. The first step is to want to be transformed. The next step is to believe that you can be transformed, by the renewing of your mind.

Chapter 7

Renewing your mind

Do not conform any longer to the pattern of this world, but be transformed by the renewing of your mind. Then, you will be able to test and approve what God's will is—His good, pleasing and perfect will. Romans 12:2

The benefits that result from mind renewal are endless. Being transformed is an interesting concept. Transformation is defined by Webster as a marked change in appearance or character, usually for the better. It's radical change. Another definition is a process of profound and radical change that orients in a new direction, taken to an entirely different level of effectiveness; a turnaround with little or no resemblance to the past configuration or structure.

Picture yourself transformed. Take a minute to stop reading and think about what you would be like if you were transformed. Maybe you should take a moment to write it down. Try writing it this way: My new life as a transformed person, with my mind renewed, discerning God's perfect will and living in perfect peace would be like this: … In "Christianese" this is a part of what is termed the sanctification process. Sanctification is the ongoing process of surrendering your soul (mind, will, emotions) in cooperation with the work of the Holy Spirit within you; internal renewal.

If your mind is renewed, your thinking will be totally different. Remember the old definition of insanity? Doing the same thing the same way and expecting a different result? If nothing changes in your thinking, nothing changes in your behavior, and nothing changes in your environment. Where does your change begin? It always begins in your mind. The "soulish" realm of your being is comprised of your mind, your will and your emotions. The three are tied up into a neat little package. Each influences the other. You already know that you are body, soul and spirit. Your soul is the thermostat of your life. Your soul dictates the direction that the rest of you navigates. You want your spirit to be intricately embedded in your soul life, but right now we are focusing on your soul alone. We will talk about your spirit later.

In the book of James (1:15), we are told that when a wrong desire is conceived in us, it then gives birth to sin. He goes on to say that when sin is fully developed it gives birth to death. Desire, sin and death: a sequence that is depicted over and over in the Bible, beginning with Eve in the garden. Our problems begin in our mind. We think about things and often let our imaginations or wrong desires run rampant. The desire moves to our emotions and we entertain it there for awhile. Then, our will gets involved. If it's something we really want to do, our will grows weak and we let it go untended.

Wrong thinking leads us down a path that is destructive. We can all cite examples of those you have watched go astray and it all started with wrong attitudes, information or desires. The point is that when you allow the Holy Spirit to guide your thoughts and you make an intentional decision to be submitted to Him, your mind begins the renewal process.

Confession of sin is a cleansing process. When we confess and repent and submit to God, a transforming process begins to move us in the right direction. Remember that self control or self discipline is a fruit of the Spirit. (Gal 5:22). Fruit is the visible evidence produced by living a Holy Spirit-led life.

The instant a wrong or negative thought comes into your mind, your self-discipline must slam on the brakes. Entertaining those thoughts for even a few seconds can send you down the declining spiral to the bottom. An important scripture to memorize is 2 Corinthians 10:5 where Paul instructs us to "take captive every thought to make it obedient to Christ." This is self-control at its best!

I go through this teaching with my counseling clients all the time. What they usually tell me is that I don't understand how fast the tapes play in their heads. Oh, but I do! When a person is wounded, surviving some type of trauma, the negative, hurtful thoughts spin out of control, sometimes constantly. Stopping those thoughts seems impossible at times. I remember in the early stages of trying to change my negative thinking patterns, I would literally have to speak out loud to get my mind to stop and change directions. I felt silly, but it worked! I would say, "Okay, stop! I am not going to think about this right now in this way. I am taking every thought captive and that means I have self-control!" I would put on some praise music and start singing with it, or I would pick up something to read---right then. The more you practice stopping the thoughts, the easier it gets. You do not have to be a victim of your own mind!

The other common mistake we make is crawling into bed at night, weary from our busy days, and using that time to meditate on our problems. The kids are finally asleep, no one will call to interrupt our thoughts and it's dark and quiet. We start thinking about all the struggles of the day, and we become more and more awake, stirring up emotions and soon, we have to get up and do something, or cry ourselves to sleep. This is a disastrous way to deal with issues. Please don't allow your mind to go there at bedtime. What you need most during stressful times is good, deep, restful sleep. So, get into bed, read something calming, think good thoughts and tell yourself when tempted to start problem solving, that you will do that in the morning, with a refreshed mind and outlook. More self-control. We all know that things always seem worse late at night when we're tired, and decisions made at 2 a.m. usually are not wise ones. Rest! In Him! Say a prayer, releasing it all to your Father, who never sleeps and is watching over you all night, and then snuggle down and rest. (Psalm 121:1-5)

'Do not conform any longer to the pattern of this world' is the beginning of that scripture. What is the pattern of this world that we are conforming to? The pattern

that says it's all about me. The pattern says if I'm not happy, happy, happy and rich and famous and skinny and gorgeous, then life is not worth living. That pattern. That pattern is not scriptural. It is never what God said about who you are to be. Dissatisfaction comes from the world. Do you live with a world view or a biblical view of what life is to be? When we try to live as Christians with a worldly outlook, we have a painful tug-of-war in our souls. I can't adequately address this topic in the scope of this book, but I can promise you that if you love the world and what it offers, this is the root of your struggle with depression, discouragement and anxiety. As Christians we are to be in the world, but not "of the world." (John 15:19) If we are immersed in the culture of money, sex and more, more, more, we are carnal Christians and totally displeasing to God.

Living a life submitted to the Holy Spirit empowers us to live a deeper existence, where holiness and godliness matter more than anything the world has to offer. Our riches in glory will come later, and we will enjoy them for all eternity. And, they will not be tied to corruption, lasciviousness or greed. But, our peace while living on this earth is also attainable, when we walk by the Spirit and rest in Him, trusting in His promises and in His provision instead of working so hard, the world's way, to try to make things happen.

The soul is a powerful segment of our makeup. It controls who we are. The beliefs we hold onto become our body's engine, transporting us daily in the direction those beliefs are geared. Contrary to popular secular psychology, this power is not totally "within us". We most definitely have choices to make and God gives us that freedom to choose, but without the Holy Spirit indwelling us, our choices will always be based on whatever knowledge we have accumulated. That knowledge can be faulty and is affected by the emotions tied to it. We see people who are in therapy for years, and still have not found the healing or freedom to live in victory. They dig and dig to find that special revelation that is hidden within them, but never hit gold.

We have lies embedded in our minds and souls. We acquire those lies when something painful happens in our lives, often when we're children. The devil joins in with people and with our own flesh to agree that we are not good enough, that we're powerless, that we'll never measure up and many more. Everyone has their own. On a good day when things are going well, we know these things are not true. But, on a rough night when we're discouraged, those lies pop up to the surface and we latch back onto them, just as we always have. We must allow God to replace those lies with His truth. *"You shall know the truth, and the truth shall set you free."* John 8:32 Someone you love and respect can give you truth about yourself all day long, but it won't heal you. When God touches our mind with His truth, the mind is renewed.

Mind renewal is a very interesting thing. I've heard dozens of interpretations of what that means, but I can attest to the fact that when God gave me truth for my lies, my mind experienced renewal. I know it was renewed because those old beliefs have never returned. The pain from those memories never returned either. Only God can do that. I can't make up my mind to "be renewed" and then presto, I'm changed. Only the Master's touch can perform the supernatural and pour divine healing into my heart and soul.

What does this have to do with resting in Him? If we are plagued by self-defeating thoughts and/or behaviors and distressing attitudes, we are weighed down and can never be at peace. Renewing your mind is one of the most important processes you will ever undergo, and will reap the most amazing benefits.

A good way to gauge your progress is to stop

occasionally and write down your thoughts. You don't have to keep a daily journal, although that is usually helpful. You can take a small notebook, date the page and jot down thoughts and emotions you're experiencing at different periods of the day. After a couple of weeks, go back and see what patterns you can identify. You will also begin to recognize some negative thinking, or lies you are believing about yourself when things are stressful. A trusted friend, counselor or pastor could talk with you and help you to identify ways to change these thought patterns and begin your turnaround.

Chapter 8

Our Identity in Christ

*"Moses spent forty years in the king's palace thinking
that he was somebody; then he lived forty years in the
wilderness finding out that without God he was a
nobody; finally he spent forty more years discovering
how a nobody with God can be a somebody."*

Dwight L. Moody

It was possibly the darkest day of my life. I started my day with a bustling morning routine, rushing off to work and thinking it was another, normal day. A couple hours into the workday, I received a phone call instructing me to go home immediately. There was a storm brewing and my house was the epicenter. My boss told me not to go. What did he know? Did he understand that disobedience could cost me my life? I knew that. I had been threatened many times before.

I drove, praying, nervous, unsure what faced me or how I would handle it. I walked into the two-story government subsidized apartment to mayhem. Shock set in, but the door slammed behind me before I could catch my breath and escape. Not one inch of the place was unscathed. Broken glass littered the floors, furniture was slashed to shreds, family heirlooms were in shattered piles on the chairs and tables.

Much of this memory is foggy, but I do remember lying on my back, with my head being rammed over and over against the concrete floor. I screamed until I was slapped silent. I remember neighbors looking in the windows and leaving. The last memory I have is a knife at my throat.

Eventually I did find myself in the hospital. I'm still not certain how I got there. The police told my dad they had seen murder scenes which looked better than my home did. Why would a woman who grew up in a solid, loving family end up with a knife at her throat, involved with a crazed abuser?

There is no doubt that I suffered from low self-esteem. The reasons could be many, but from my counseling experience, I know that most people have this in their life's resume at some point. It takes life's experiences to mature and grow beyond it.

I fell prey to an abusive man who as all of them do, started the relationship with flowers and poems and promises. He fed my starved emotions with all the right words and actions. This evolved into a nightmare situation within a very short time. I was emotionally, verbally and physically beaten down. I endured the vilest verbal abuse imaginable. I was accused of things I could never have even considered, much less done. I lived in fear for my life. Once I was beaten with the end of a shotgun. Time and time again I was slapped or pushed against walls. In the end, on this fateful day, I arrived at the local hospital bleeding physically and emotionally. To allow myself to be brought down to that level means there was not much knowledge of my true identity...as a child of God. Abused women begin to believe this is normal life and often take years to find their freedom from it. I praise God that through the love of family and friends, and most of all my Lord, I found a way out before it was too late.

For me to begin to believe in myself and in all that God had planned for me, it was necessary to study the scriptures and apply them daily to my thinking and my behaviors. Slowly over time, my confidence grew, both in myself and in my God. He showed me so many wonderful truths about His plans for me, His love for me and who I am in Him. Jesus living in me means I hold a power beyond any mortal man's physical strength. I just have to appropriate that power and let Him rule over all. I must always be in full cooperation with His Spirit and fully submitted to His leading in order to live that life of enjoying my identity in Christ. This comes over time. I believe this is a journey most young adults walk as they find out who they are and especially who God called them to be. It took a tragic year of my life to begin to understand the importance of knowing my identity in Christ.

Another important aspect of learning to rest in God is being at peace with who we are. When I ask clients to write about who they are, they almost always list roles, such as mother, teacher, artist and so on. Who you are is not what you do. Those roles you fill, of course, are intricately tied to who you are, but those roles are not the real "you." Your identity is who you are on the inside, your character and nature. You must be secure in your knowledge of who you are to be able to live in peace. Many people base their interpretation of who they are on how others see them. That is a slippery slope. It means that if those who love you and express approval and acceptance are around, you are feeling fine. But, if someone comes along who has a criticism of you, you are deflated and discouraged. This is no way to live! It becomes a roller coaster ride of life that causes you to live by emotions. Up one day; down the next. How can you rest in God, living a life of peace, if your whole perception of yourself depends on someone's critique de jour?

Once again I can point you to many scriptures which confirm that our identity is in Christ alone. (See Appendix A) When we submit our lives to Christ and He lives within us, the Bible teaches us that we automatically inherit a new identity that is based in Him. It means that as long as we are living according to His Word, submitted to Him and to godly living, it does not matter what any person's opinion of us is. Yes, we always want to make a good impression, set a good example, and we naturally want people to like us and respect us. However, we all know people who may not do either, who do not share our values and their opinion does not in any way negate who we are! We must be able to stand firm and say "I'm disappointed that you do not like me or agree with me, but this is where I stand." The next step is the critical one: walk away feeling confident and unstressed. Like anything else, it takes practice. It takes prayer as well. The Lord will help you learn to walk in confidence regarding who you are. Your identity is in Him, not in the world or who the world says you should be.

I love this quote from Nouwen:

> *"When we are spiritually free, we do not have to worry about what to say or do in unexpected, difficult circumstances. When we are not concerned about what others think of us or what we will get for what we do, the right words and actions will emerge from the centre of our beings because the Spirit of God, who makes us children of God and sets us free, will speak and act through us." Henri J. M. Nouwen*

I learned so much from Dr. Neil Anderson through his book, "Victory over the Darkness." He offers concise teaching, explaining that you cannot earn your qualities of life any more than you earn your salvation. He states "The more you affirm who you are in Christ, the more your behavior will reflect your true identity." The level of peace that resides within you is directly related to your confidence level; your security level of your true identity. The more confidence you have, the more peace you have. When your confidence is not defined by others' opinions and attitudes, or by the world's standards of achievement, you will be tucked securely in His rest.

Some people report that progress in this area comes by first pretending to be confident and strong even when you don't feel it or believe it. Repeating God's promises as affirmations builds strength within. You will be surprised how practice brings confidence, affirming and believing what God's word says about you.

I've spent years working with women who have been abused by spouses or other adults. What I've heard so many times is that the abuser emotionally and verbally beats them down by repeating negative slurs so much that the woman begins to question herself and often starts believing the curses. This goes back to our discussion on renewing our minds. We often curse ourselves by thinking and saying negative statements about ourselves. The more we think it or say it, the more embedded it becomes into our psyche. And, again, what we think is who we become.

Our identity as a vessel with Christ living in us changes everything. The power at work in us is indescribable. But only if we use it. If a robber breaks into your home and you are standing there with a gun in your hand, but never use it, the intruder will probably overtake you and do whatever his evil intent is to do.

You are holding the power, but you must engage it for it to be beneficial.

I can be so happy to know that Christ lives in me, that I am indwelt by the Holy Spirit of God, but if I constantly speak curses over myself, telling myself and those around me just how useless I am, no power is activated. Does that mean I should not be humble? Not at all. Jesus was very humble, but He walked in confidence and strength.

Children's development also depends strongly on what is spoken over them and about them. Speaking blessings into their lives on a regular basis will produce fruit in their lives that is positive and inspiring. Speaking curses over them will deflate and discourage them. Both have outcomes that are evident as they grow into adulthood. Speaking blessings will assist in developing their identity, hopefully rooted and grounded in Christ as well. *"Death and life are in the power of the tongue"* (Proverbs 18:21).

"Today I have given you the choice between life and death, between blessings and curses. Now I call on heaven and earth to witness the choice you make. Oh, that you would choose life, so that you and your descendants might live!" Deuteronomy 30:19

Choose life! Life in Christ is true freedom because He

is the One at work within you. Your identity in Him means that you have activated His power in your life and chosen to walk in confidence and strength.

After my abuse experience, my life began a transformation. God had a plan that was beyond anything I could have ever imagined. One night I was in tears, crying out to God about how sorry I was for wasting so many years and rebelling in so many ways. He spoke to me gently, "Not one part of your life is wasted. I use it all to form you into the person I've planned for you to be from the beginning." What a healing answer for my soul. My identity in Him means that He's in control; He's in charge of my progress, my purpose and my future. It leaves my self-worth in His hands, not mine. That, to me, is the ultimate security. Resting in my identity in Him causes me to walk in confidence and wisdom never known before.

> *"Just think, you are here not by chance but by GOD's choosing. His hand formed you and made you the person you are. He compares you to no one else; you are one of a kind. You lack nothing that His grace can't give you. He has allowed you to be here at this time in history to fulfill His special purpose for this generation. You are GOD's servant in GOD's place at GOD's perfect time." Roy Lessin*

Chapter 9

Spiritual Roots of Physical Distress

Learning to live in God's rest can improve your physical health as well as your emotional and spiritual well-being. There is an interesting phenomenon that occurs when we endure long, stressful seasons of our lives. The immune system of our physical bodies begins to disintegrate at a slow rate, but ostensibly is weakening to the point that we become susceptible to contracting all kinds of viruses. As if this isn't bad enough, research shows that if high stress levels continue over a sustained period of time, other organs of the body weaken and disease has an open door.

I began studying spiritual/emotional roots of disease about ten years ago. At the outset, I was skeptical about the items I was reading. The teachings were authored by Christians but the biblical references seemed vague and were possibly stretched a bit more than I felt comfortable with. However, over time and extended study, I began to change my mind about the results.

I started by compiling a list of spiritual and emotional problems that result in specific illnesses. For example, unforgivenesss and bitterness were said to produce arthritis and other joint dysfunctions. Each condition was listed with an emotional or spiritual cause. I dug out a stack of old files from counseling clients, who, at intake, had listed their physical histories and medications they were taking. They were seeing me for emotional and spiritual issues. I was shocked to find the match of the clients' physical diagnoses to their presenting emotional/spiritual issues were astoundingly about 90% in line with the studies. I began to take a little different approach with clients as they came for ministry, based on this information. I was amazed at the success rate of those who submitted to prayer for inner healing and for their emotional and spiritual needs, watching their physical problems either disappear or dramatically improve.

God created us in the most awesome manner, connecting body, soul and spirit. When one part is sick, the other two suffer as well. Am I saying that every time you get sick, you are doing something wrong, that you are in sin? NO!! There are illnesses and diseases that stem from environmental causes and other roots as well. However, remember that in the book of James, we are taught that when we go to the elders or leaders for them to anoint us with oil and pray for our healing, he tells us to first confess our sins, that we may be healed. Obviously, that opens the door for the strong possibility that many illnesses are rooted in sin. Now, that being said, I want to explain this in a deeper sense.

Worry and anxiety wear the body down. They wear the soul and spirit down as well. They are sin. We usually excuse those sins because we have a good reason to be worried or stressed or anxious. Right? Today, in our culture, people almost boast about the level of stress and anxiety they experience on a daily basis. It's almost a badge of honor, proving we are working hard or achieving something. It is so prevalent that no one thinks anything about it except that it's a normal part of everyday life and if you have to live on medication for it, you accept it. That is pretty much the secular viewpoint. Of course, a small amount of stress can be a positive thing, but most of us tend to teeter off the scale of healthy stress. Stress is only one example of an emotional root of illness. There are countless others, but the immune system is most affected by fear, anxiety and stress.

I was in the midst of studying the spiritual/emotional roots of disease when I had an eye-opening experience. One morning I began to think about my diagnosis of hypothyroidism. I had been diagnosed at age ten and had been on medication for it since. I researched the emotional root and learned that it was based in self hatred or self rejection. This disturbed me. I prayed and said, "Lord, I do not hate myself; what is this about?" I heard the Lord speak to me, "Stop cursing your body." I was stunned. I thought about it for a few seconds and said, "Lord, I don't curse my body." In a flash, my own words began flooding my mind. "I'm so ugly. I'm so fat. My legs are hideous. My feet are repulsive." The deluge continued for a few minutes until I was in tears. I had no idea I had been cursing my body. It certainly sounded like self hatred. I would never have seen that for myself; obviously not, since it had gone on for most of my life. I promised the Lord that day that I would stop cursing my body and begin blessing it. It was excruciatingly difficult and did not happen overnight. However, over time

I was able to think and verbalize positive blessings about myself.

One day I was praying and God showed me I was healed of hypothyroidism. I was so excited I was dancing around my house. I made an appointment with my doctor for testing. I had to be off my medication for ten days before the test. The test indicated a perfectly normal thyroid function. The doctor was doubtful. She insisted that something must have interfered with my test because there is no cure for hypothyroidism and no one outgrows it. She instructed me to wait awhile and be retested.

A few months later while having an annual physical exam, my thyroid function was once again tested thoroughly, and the results were normal again. I am still praising God for this healing because it not only healed my physical condition, but healed emotional and spiritual issues that were unhealthy and unholy. I had to learn to love myself. It was *work*. It was reaching into a depth of my soul that was painful. The level of honesty with myself and God was more than humbling. But…it was worth every second.

Ask God to help you be mindful of your patterns of speaking blessings or curses. Do you love yourself or reject yourself? This concept has had such an impact on my life and I have no doubt that the spirit realm is also engaged as these words and attitudes project into the atmosphere. We call down angels to surround our situation, or we can open doors to demons by speaking curses. Are we agreeing with God, our Creator, or are we agreeing with the enemy of our soul, who is out to destroy us?

Don't be afraid to take an inventory, exploring your current attitudes, behaviors and problems to identify how the wounds of your past are affecting your life today. You do not have to suppress your pain. You can stuff it and say you've dealt with it, but your behaviors and your physical health will expose the truth. On the other side of the coin, did you know that laughter can strengthen your immune system? It has been documented that laughter causes the body to manufacture T cells and killer cells that fight cancer.

A merry heart doeth good like a medicine, but a broken spirit drieth the bones. Proverbs 17:22

"Researchers found that when happy people contract a virus, or "catch a cold", they report fewer symptoms and in fact, are less likely to contract the virus at all. This recent study confirms an earlier finding by Carnegie Mellon University Psychology Professor

Sheldon Cohen, in which he found people who are happy, lively, calm or exhibit other positive emotions are less likely to become ill when they are exposed to a cold virus than those who report few of these emotions." Rick Nauert, PhD

It's not just a matter of positive thinking. It is a matter of changing your thought patterns to align with your emotions. Getting healing for your emotions will cause a domino effect that will lead to your body responding with better health. Suppressing emotions uses up a lot of energy, which robs your body of energy that should be used for vital functions. Negative emotions tax your adrenal glands and use up nutrients the body needs to sustain itself. The result is fatigue and lowered vitality.

I would also like to impress upon you that if, in reading this, you identify with some of these examples, please do not start beating yourself up with guilt or shame. That will only bring about more issues that need healing. *"There is now therefore no condemnation for those who are in Christ Jesus."* Romans 8:1. Self-condemnation is not the plan Jesus has for you, and He will lead you out of your wrong thinking and your emotional pain. He will do it gently, so you need to be gentle with yourself as well.

In the next chapter we will address some deeper emotional issues and how they affect our peace. I hope you're beginning to understand the impact our attitudes have upon our physical and spiritual health and our ability to live in His rest.

Chapter 10

Damaged Emotions and God's Rest

The LORD is my light and my salvation; whom shall I fear? The LORD is the strength of my life; of whom shall I be afraid? When the wicked, even mine enemies and my foes, came upon me to eat up my flesh, they stumbled and fell. Though an host should encamp against me, my heart shall not fear: though war should rise against me, in this will I be confident. Psalm 27:1-3

Fear: The greatest paralyzer and stealer of peace

What are you afraid of? Fear is the most paralyzing force known to mankind. There are over 530 documented phobias people have reported over the years. You can probably name at least ten, and you possibly have a few in your own closet. There is even a phobia called phobophobia, a fear of phobias! A list of more interesting fears that gave me a chuckle were:

Trichopathophobia - Fear of hair
Peladophobia - Fear of bald people.
Melophobia - Fear of music
Lachanophobia - Fear of vegetables.
Hippopotomonstrosesquippedaliophobia   - Fear of long words (can you even pronounce that word?)
Arachibutyrophobia - Fear of peanut butter getting stuck to the roof of your mouth.
Unatractiphobia - Fear of ugly people.
Dromophobia - Fear of crossing the road.
Pogonophobia - Fear of beards.
Linonophobia - Fear of string.
(http://www.kidzworld.com/article/2052)

According to most studies, death is the second greatest fear on the long, long list (number one is public speaking). It has also been said that every fear is connected to the ultimate fear of death. If there is no fear of death, it obliterates so many other anxieties. As Christians, why would we fear death? We believe the life after this one is exceedingly superior to this in every facet. We value life and are not ready to walk through the valley of death prematurely, but donning a cloak of fear each day drains all abundant life from us. Death was actually defeated at the cross of Christ. We walk from this life into the new life in heaven, so only our physical bodies actually cease living; our spirits live on in greater glory.

> *"Yea, though I walk through the valley of the shadow of death, I will fear no evil: for thou art with me; thy rod and thy staff they comfort me. Thou preparest a table before me in the presence of mine enemies: thou anointest my head with oil; my cup runneth over. Psalm 23:4-5*

It's not difficult to recognize how fear steals our peace and our ability to rest in God. If we are constantly afraid of something, our productivity suffers, our sleep suffers, our overall health suffers. Fear is a relentless thief. In scripture, we are told to "fear not" over 365 times. That's at least one for each day of the year. I found at least 100 on my own. The Lord not only understands our human condition regarding fear, but He also feels compelled to keep reminding us that we do not need to be afraid.

There are countless books written on overcoming fear. Research on the internet can also reap thousands of articles on how to defeat it. I could only skim the surface of that exhaustive supply of information in this small teaching. If you suffer from fear, take the time to educate yourself with some of these studies. They can prove very helpful.

What I want to focus on is the fact that as you entertain fear over an extended period of time, you may possibly open doors of invitation to demonic spirits which delight in supporting your stance. A spirit of fear is a bully who has no actual power over a Christian, but masquerades as very powerful--- powerful enough to leave one quaking in the dark. It is all a game to him, to bluff you with fear tactics because you do not understand your identity in Christ, which empowers you to overcome any ploy he uses. We will talk more about spiritual warfare later, but it's important at this point to understand that if the enemy of your soul can paralyze you with fear, he ostensibly has you defeated from whatever call God has on your life.

To backtrack just a little, we see many instances

where fear is a generational curse. We can listen to stories about how our great, great grandmother performed certain rituals to ward off fear, or family history relating anecdotes about relatives who exhibited amusing traits, all related to fear. Some share about their parents or grandparents using fear as a disciplinary measure.

It gets passed along for generations and usually is unintentional, but damaging just the same. We need to pray and ask God to break those generational curses once and for all, as we learn to live by faith and trust in Him, not dependent on fearful rituals or faulty thinking any longer.

Often my clients who deal with paralyzing fear, share about their daily struggles with fear of the dark, fear of being alone, fear of attackers, intruders or crime. Many of them have histories of watching horror movies, violent crime stories on television, and reading science fiction terror plots. God's Word says in Psalm 101:3 *"I will set before my eyes no vile thing. The deeds of faithless men I hate; they will not cling to me."* Opening up our minds to vile things can also open our spirits to fear. Those plots will often 'cling' to your mind and spirit. I am heartbroken when I work with children who have had no parental supervision when it comes to their television, movie and book choices. Children's natural curiosity will guide them directly into those scary areas, which appear exciting to them, but bring about some terrible consequences to their little souls. And again, those spirits of fear often are brought in when a child is small, and then continue to torment a person throughout adulthood, if not dealt with.

The spirit world is very real. Many people choose to ignore it, deny it or have a fear of learning about it. The Bible is clear about it and teaches us all we need to know about dealing with it and standing strong above fear and intimidation. 2 Timothy 1:7 states, *"God has not given us a spirit of fear, but of power, love and a sound mind."* Sometimes, in a period of tremendous fear, we don't feel that our mind is sound, but we must remember that God Himself is living within us, promising us a sound mind and the love and the power to defeat any attacks of the enemy.

The key to overcoming fear is to understand the power that is within you, namely Jesus Christ, and when you fully understand His power at work in you, you can then command a spirit of fear to leave once and for all, and it will be gone...forever. If this spirit knows that you don't know Christ's power and that you have tons of doubt and unbelief, it will continue harassing you. This is an important revelation to grab hold of.

Study and pray to lose all doubt and unbelief so that you put on the whole armor of God and having done all, to stand! (Ephesians 6:10-18). Someone once said, "Do the thing you fear most and the death of fear is certain." If having a stand-off with a demon of fear is what you fear most, do it! God is your protector and He says the battle is His. Let Him win it for you and through you. It is possible. You must believe it is possible.

If your battle with fear does not seem to be demonic, but more about your own insecurities, remember the battle begins in your mind and how you choose to think determines your behavior.

> *"Our lives are full of supposes. Suppose this should happen, or suppose that should happen; what could we do; how could we bear it? But, if we are living in the high tower of the dwelling place of God, all these supposes will drop out of our lives. We shall be quiet from the fear of evil, for no threatenings of evil can penetrate into the high tower of God. " Hannah Whitall Smith*

Depression

Recently, a friend called me to chat. She remarked how angry she was because she heard a pastor on a radio show saying that depression was a sin against God. She interpreted that to mean that Christians should never be depressed and that if we were, we were bad Christians. We talked at length about it. No one walks the perfect Christian life. We do our best but we all fall short. We decided, after much discussion, that while we never want to put anyone under condemnation, the truth is that the standard we would want to achieve, according to scripture, would be to never be in depression. There are many standards in God's Word that we, as humans, never reach, but they remain to be what we strive for. If we are living a Spirit filled life, a life of trusting totally in God and following His teaching and the counsel of the Holy Spirit we would not fall prey to all the stresses that lead there. Does that mean we never have a down day or never get sad or stressed when things are rough? Absolutely not! God gave us emotions and experiencing emotions is vital to a healthy life. But, continuing on in a depressed state over a period of time (probably more than a couple of weeks) means that one needs to get some help to determine the root and get rid of it.

Prolonged discouragement and depression indicates some wrong thinking somewhere. It doesn't mean that you have not been mistreated, or misjudged or that you do not have reason to be hurting. It means that you have not learned to take that particular hurt and find healing for it.

We've all heard the old adage that depression is anger turned inward. Is there some deeply rooted anger that you have not dealt with? Sometimes we are forced to live through a trial that seems to make no sense. Our natural tendency is to make our case to God: "Lord, I've given money to the poor, I've taught Sunday School, I've lived by your Word the best I know how,..." on and on we go. So, the biggest question is "why?" Why did I lose my job? Why was I lied to and betrayed by my best friend? Why was I diagnosed with this disease? We may get answers, and then again, we may not. Either way, it's normal to get angry. There's obviously a good reason to be angry. The problem comes when we stay angry and do not resolve it within ourselves and with God. Perhaps the anger is toward God. Talk to Him about it. He knows your every thought anyway.

Mother Teresa once said that depression is the ultimate form of self-centeredness. Ouch. That one really stings. But, there is a chance that too much focus on self and other inward focusing thoughts has gotten out of control. The disappointment you've suffered eats away at your attitudes and thinking until the negativity feels normal. Perhaps you have had unrealistic expectations in some area, or plans or desires that do not line up with God's plan for you. His plan is always best, though we can be stubborn in pursuing our own ideas for years at a time, not realizing we're heading in a wrong direction. Then we can't figure out why we are not happy or fulfilled. This goes back to our discussion about trusting Him. His love is magnificent! It might require time to stop and pray and discover if some desires you have are God-given or world-driven. Or maybe your disappointment stems from believing you were planning something great to do for God, but it hasn't panned out.

Our disappointments generally are rooted in a self-focus. It may not be obvious. The best thing to try in this case is to ask yourself what would be in it for you, even if the plan was to do for others in some area. Without that plan, fill in the blank for how it makes you feel to be without it. Go beyond angry, sad or disappointed. Dig deeper for an emotion that would surface, showing the unhealed wound in yourself that needed that plan to fulfill you. If it's a deep hurt, you might need a counselor or pastor to help you walk through the process.

Others have shared with me that since their doctors told them they would live on anti-depressants for the rest of their lives, due to chemical imbalances, they lost all motivation to conquer the depression. Chemical imbalances are generally due to decreased serotonin levels. Serotonin is generated by adrenaline circulating in a healthy mind/body interaction. When negativity and emotional pain wear it down, the lack of it keeps a person feeling down and out. That is, of course, a very simplified version of how the body's chemistry ends up when one is in depression. You can research this on your own and get a better, clearer understanding of how the body chemistry operates. My point is that if your body can become chemically imbalanced from lack of serotonin, and serotonin can be regenerated, then you do not have to accept a life sentence of depression. Can your God, who created your body, not regenerate the necessary levels of serotonin in your body? He can remove all chemical imbalances.

You can play a major role in that regenerative process by changing attitudes and renewing your mind. When your thought processes begin to change, it has a chain reaction. As you think more positively, you begin to feel happier, which transfers to your physical health, thus, most likely, ending your depression. Many people have shared testimonies of how change in their thought processes produced emotional as well as physical healing, leaving them free from depression. I find that those who get angry or defensive about their depression are generally those who have some deeply held belief that they have some right to hold onto it. Or, there are those who simply find it easier to depend on the medication and leave life as it is. Please do not misunderstand me. I have genuine compassion for those struggling with depression. I have been there, more than once. I simply know that my *"God is able to do exceedingly, abundantly, far more, than we can ever ask or imagine."* (Ephesians 3:20) There is no condemnation; only hope and opportunity.

Unforgiveness

Another issue that plagues our ability to enter His rest is unforgiveness. We know that in order to be forgiven by God, we must forgive others. This is God's rule, not mine. He has a solid reason for requiring that. When you have carried resentments from your wounds, you know that they weigh you down. Resentments fester and eventually turn into bitterness. Who enjoys the company of a bitter person? Even the bitter person does not love her own company! Holding grudges and being bound to offenses only deepens your wounds, blocking healing.

Sometimes people say that staying angry provides some barrier from ever being hurt again. What a lie that is! If anything, it will lead to more hurt because people react to your anger which can have a domino effect in destroying relationships. Many times we say we have forgiven someone, but we cringe thinking of a surprise encounter in a store, or feel a tinge of anger when we hear about a success that person is enjoying. Maybe you've heard the saying that *"holding onto unforgiveness is like drinking poison and waiting for the other person to die." Carrie Fisher*

A good test of whether you have forgiven is to pray for that person and honestly ask God to bless them. Follow that up with asking God's forgiveness for you for judging that person. When you mean it, you are free. You are not doing it for them---you're doing it for you, and for God! He gave you the ability to forgive. Ask Him to help you do it. Forgiving is like cutting the chains and being lifted out of the swamp to spread wings and soar! Does it excuse the wrongs which hurt you? No. It means that you have relinquished the person and their behaviors and attitudes to God and He will deal with that for you. It's out of your hands. You're free! Every piece of truth you acquire moves you one step closer to the person God has purposed for you to be. And in essence, you have entered into His rest, at peace with yourself, others and your God.

As we learned in the preceding chapter, much research has been carried on over the past few years indicating that unforgiveness and bitterness can lead to joint problems, such as arthritis. A woman shared with me that she once had been burdened with crippling osteoarthritis, deforming her hands and causing her much pain. After going through some serious inner healing ministry, forgiving some horrendous acts of abuse in her childhood, this precious lady saw her fingers straighten out and her pain disappear. It was truly a miracle that only God could perform!

Whenever my joints begin to hurt, I always ask the Lord to reveal if I am carrying any resentment toward anyone and often He shows me someone I need to forgive. As I release that person to His charge, my pain subsides. Once again, I know there are other causes of arthritis, but isn't it a blessing that we can go to our Lord and His promises for healing, trusting in Him, and it doesn't cost us a penny. It might cost some pride, however.

A few years back, I went through a deeply painful experience when my closest friend and ministry partner betrayed me. This was a person I looked up to, shared my deepest thoughts with, prayed with and our families spent hours together as well. The hurt was deep and I'm sorry to say it took me years to get free from the pain of that betrayal. One day I realized that holding on to that hurt and resentment was not only hurting me, but in some ways it could also be a curse on her. I also realized I did not want that. My judgment of her was a sin as well as holding onto my resentment. I am so thankful that God gave me the ability to let go and completely forgive this person because I am the one who is free. I have no idea if she ever repented or not. I hope so. I only know that it took a heavy weight off my heart.

A scripture that the Lord has given me many times, is Isaiah 30:15 *"In repentance and rest is your salvation, in quietness and trust is your strength."* Perhaps after reading this, you can see a reason for you to take some time to assess your current mode of operation and ask yourself if you have taken time to repent of stinkin' thinkin' and begin to flush out the spiritual roots of your physical problems. Take some time to meditate on these things, and get serious in seeking the Lord's direction about healing. Stomp out that pride and talk with someone who will help you find healing for your emotional and spiritual issues, so that your body can heal too.

Living in God's rest requires an act of submission on your part. Submitting your right to be angry, your right to stay depressed, your right to hold onto whatever stronghold is actually blocking His rest from you. Relinquish all your rights to your fleshly hang-ups, and run into the arms of God where His love will envelop you, body, soul and spirit.

Chapter 11

What does change look like?

How would your life look different today if you were living in His rest? My client, Amy, (not her real name) agreed to share her testimony.

Amy got up early one morning, breaking her usual routine, carrying a steaming cup of coffee and her Bible out onto her flower-lined deck. She had made the decision last night to make some major changes in her routine. Working forty plus hours a week and parenting two adolescents took a lot of energy. Her husband, Chuck, drove a truck and often wasn't home for weeks at a time. It was much like being a single parent. Just last week, Amy's doctor informed her that she must make some critical changes or her health was sure to decline quickly. Her blood pressure was higher than ever, her headaches were steadily escalating, and she was not sleeping well at all. Amy tried so hard not to worry. Her kids each had specific issues that took time and energy to deal with. Chuck was a good provider, but was emotionally absent when he was finally physically present. And, her mother was recently diagnosed with cancer. Amy was tired. She sat, this cool spring morning, sipping her coffee as the sun was rising and looked at the scriptures in front of her. "God, do you really see my life? Do you really care that I am exhausted and see no changes ahead that can relieve my busy, stressful life?" She looked down at a Psalm, jumping off the page. Psalm 139:2 *"you know when I sit and when I rise,....you are familiar with all my ways....before a word is on my tongue, you know it completely, O Lord."* Okay, Amy thought, I know that You know absolutely everything about me and my life. So, why is my life so hard? If you are a God of love and compassion and you know all about me, why am I so stressed and why doesn't life get better? As if He was whispering in her ear, Amy heard in her spirit, the words of Matthew 11:28: *"come to me, all you who are weary and burdened, and I will give you rest.... you will find rest for your soul."* She relaxed a little and thought, "maybe I don't really come to You and maybe I don't really lay my burdens in your lap. But I certainly want to, Lord! Show me how!"

Amy is like so many of us. We know what the scriptures say, but we forget, in our hectic busy-ness, to stop and hand it all over to Him. He is waiting and more than willing to take it all off our shoulders, but we don't let Him. We ask Him for help, but we don't change anything we're doing or any of our ways of thinking, so like that old definition of insanity, the results remain the same.

Amy made an intentional decision to change her life. She examined her daily routine, but more importantly than that, she made an honest assessment of her thought life. She realized that her self-talk was often negative and hopeless. She even heard her children saying they were tired much more often than children normally would and she knew they were picking up her bad habits. She was modeling a defeated, tired mom and wife with a sense of hopelessness. She knew this was not what the Christian life was supposed to be about.

Amy memorized 2 Corinthians 10:5 making a commitment to *"take every thought captive to the obedience of Christ."* Changing her thoughts and words was not easy. The problems in her life were still very real. Sometimes it felt like three steps forward and two steps backward. Thoughts of giving up came and went. She prayed and stayed focused on taking every thought captive, not allowing the negativity to overtake her. Over a period of a few weeks, Amy began to see some remarkable changes. She was feeling lighter and more hopeful. She was careful to thank God and continue seeking Him on a daily basis. She researched scriptures that related to trust, hope, faith and yes, rest. She posted a different verse on her refrigerator each week and her children joined her in memorizing them. She shared with friends that she was amazed at how God was replacing her discouragement and weariness with a fresh hope and calmness. Peace in the midst of her storms. She made new efforts to go to bed at the same time each night and refused to think about her problems before going to sleep. Within three months, Amy was sleeping all night, her blood pressure was back to normal and she had more energy. It was well worth her hard fought efforts to make the changes. Her husband was still gone a lot; her mother was still sick; her job continued to be hard, and her children had their issues. However, Amy was gaining a new perception of the inner peace that was taking over and could feel it, not only in her mind, but in a more relaxed body as well. She is now trusting God more, believing He will work all things together for good, and as a result, she is much closer now to living in God's rest.

Every small step you take toward living in His rest will reap rewards. Pay close attention to your words so that you can realize patterns of negativity and unbelief. Our words are projected into the atmosphere and can alight on our children or coworkers causing a cloud of doubt affecting each person. How does God, our Father feel when we constantly voice doubt and unbelief? We are instructed to walk by faith, and pray in faith, believing! Believing that His plan is good and His promises are true. Every time we verbalize negative thoughts which contradict the words of the

Lord, we are in effect, coming into agreement with the enemy. That's not what we want to do. The more often we are agreeing with the enemy, the more often we see ourselves spiraling downward into despair and depression.

Speaking life into situations by declaring God's word will validate and affirm them to your mind and your emotions and behavior will follow. Just like Amy, it begins with a commitment to making a change and then is followed up with action. Always pray and ask the Lord to help you, strengthen your emotions and quicken your spirit when you are heading in the wrong direction. He will gently guide you into all truth. He longs to shelter you in His arms and strengthen you to walk in freedom.

Here is a prayer that might be helpful as you assess your need for change.

Father, I am so thankful that I can come to You to learn how to enter Your rest. Please help me to be strong in the power of Your might, trusting Your guidance and direction as I make changes in my thinking and behaviors. Please help me to take every thought captive to Your will. Help me to stop my negative thought patterns and replace them with your promises. I renounce all my doubt and unbelief, and from this day forward I will choose to have faith in Your promises for my life. I thank you in advance, trusting that You will fill me with Your Spirit and encourage me daily. In Jesus' name, Amen.

Chapter 12

What about the devil?

*Be self-controlled and alert. Your enemy
the devil prowls around like a roaring lion
looking for someone to devour. 1 Peter 5:8*

One important aspect of learning to live in God's rest is recognizing the spiritual warfare going on around us. We live in a cursed creation, with the god of this world, namely satan, hard at work. There is a reason he is called the enemy of your soul. He prowls around looking for someone to devour. Satan is not out to make your life difficult; he is out to destroy it. Never forget that. If he cannot take you down one way, he will seek out another one. One of his greatest ploys in today's culture is to attack our minds, planting deception, and then go to his next prey, waiting for us to self-destruct. We latch onto his lies and let them take us down. We aren't alert to the fact that we're being deceived because he attacks us through hurt and disappointments in our lives and when our guard is down, we are susceptible to agreeing with him.

The Bible teaches us *"the weapons of our warfare are not physical. They are spiritual, and they are mighty before God for the pulling down of strongholds." (2 Corinthians 10:4)* That's a mouthful of scripture that might be cloudy to some.

First, what is a stronghold and why does it need to be pulled down? The definition of stronghold is: A place of survival or security. A stronghold is a fortress, a wall built solidly enough to withstand attacks. There are numerous applications to illustrate what a stronghold can be, but in this particular case, it is an entrenched belief so firmly established in your mind that you cannot just decide one minute to change it, and it's changed in the next breath. This is an attitude that is set in stone, an addiction, a false belief or understanding, or a sin of any type that is standing firm and secure unless some major, life-changing mind renewal happens. It's usually there because you have suffered some deep hurt or offense that caused you to erect that wall in defense of your soul.

As a Christian, you may even be aware that it needs to come down, but you feel you don't have what it takes to attack such a monumental job. In our efforts to understand this scripture, we are told the weapons we use to pull down those strongholds are not physical weapons. The only weapons that will disintegrate those strongholds are spiritual. It's a little challenging to wrap your mind around that concept. Satan and his demons are spirit beings. God and the Holy Spirit are Spirit beings. You have a spirit and hopefully it is saturated and indwelt by God's Holy Spirit. Therefore, the power that is in you (God) which is greater than the one that is in the world (satan), is The One which can demolish your strongholds. You just have to cooperate.....by surrendering your will and trusting in His.

This takes us back to mind renewal. As we battle to change our thinking and attitudes so we can live in God's rest, anxiety-free, we would be remiss if we did not include spiritual warfare as part of our training. Spiritual warfare is not about exhausting ourselves fighting demons. The apostle Paul, after instructing us how to put on the whole armor of God when the enemy is attacking, says to "stand." He says, "having done all, STAND." (Ephesians 6) First, you clothe yourself in your armor, which is a piece by piece understanding of your position as a chosen child of the King of Kings, fully comprehending your identity in Christ, and then standing firm, not chasing demons around. They have already had to flee because of the power at work within you. (See Appendix B for more explanation of the whole armor of God.) So, as you find yourself standing firm, you are at the ultimate resting place, God's total rest which is perfect peace.

Did I lose you on that last spin of the tilt-a-whirl? The simplified version is this: when you are secure in your position as a chosen, forgiven, set-free child of God, you realize the *power* that is at work within you. When the enemy attacks, you stand firm, knowing that all you have to do is pray, believing (no doubt) and stand firm. God will protect you, provide for you, inspire you, and set your course for whatever action must follow. You are relaxed, trusting, and secure in the knowledge that He will never leave you or forsake you, so there is no reason for any worry, stress or anxiety. Living that way over time means your physical health will thrive. It's a partnership, but He is at the controls.

This is truth for those who have submitted their lives to the Lord. If it all sounds like gibberish to you, be aware of this scripture:

> *"The man (person) without the Spirit does not accept the things that come from the Spirit of God, for they are foolishness to him, and he cannot understand them, because they are spiritually discerned." (1 Corinthians 2:14)*

When you surrender your life to God, accepting Jesus as Lord of your life, the Holy Spirit enters your being, indwelling your spirit, and opening your eyes to the spiritual realm. This is why many cannot understand spiritual things. They do not have the Holy Spirit indwelling them. Conversely, in 2nd Peter 1:3-4 we learn that

"His divine power has given us everything we need for life and godliness through our knowledge of him who called us by his own glory and goodness.

> *Through these he has given us his very great and precious promises, so that through them you may participate in the divine nature and escape the corruption in the world caused by evil desires."*

This is only one example of the truth that we have His "divine power" at work within us, empowering us to defeat the weakness of our flesh and also to stand against attacks of the enemy.

Living in God's rest allows us to reap the rewards of

putting on that whole armor of God, standing firm in our knowledge of who we are in Him, and just relaxing in the truth. Sometimes you hear people saying they are "under attack" and often that is followed by a litany of negative circumstances that have befallen them. We can be under attack by the enemy, and truthfully if we're living for Christ, we will be attacked consistently, but this is not an excuse for whining or self-pity. This is a time for rising up in strength, to stand victorious in our power over the enemy. He is a major bluffer. He was defeated at the cross, and though he can sometimes cause damage in our lives, he is never the victor except when we allow it. Our problem is that we fall prey to the bluff. We must learn to be always alert to his schemes and resist him at every turn. It is supernatural. All the power is within us through Jesus Christ.

Let's look at an example of how this can play out. Remember that in order to have victory over the enemy, you must be submitted to God first.

You've just been to church and heard a sermon about lust. You know you have a weakness in that area. You've sincerely repented of past lustful thoughts and any resulting actions from that lust. You prayed and know that God has forgiven you and you head home feeling lighter, freer, and ready to face the world.

Before going to bed that night, you decide to check your messages on your social networking site and one of your friends has posted a link to a funny video. You think that would be a good way to end the day..... laughing. After all, it's been a good day. The video is funny, but in the middle of it a very seductive person of the opposite sex shows up with just a slight off-color suggestion. Before you realize it, you are having some old, lustful thoughts beginning to play in your mind. This scenario could go any direction, but for the person serious about standing firm in godliness, what is the next step? Crying, "that's not fair, the devil made me do it!"?

There are several ways you could handle this attack from the enemy. Preferably, you would have a plan in place ahead of time to stop a video the instant something provocative hits the screen and then immediately pray for God's help in turning away. Or, after watching it and realizing you are still very weak in that area, take the time then to go to God with it, being brutally honest. Command the demon to leave in the name of Jesus Christ and mean it. Follow that up with praying a scripture such as *"I can do all things through Christ who strengthens me"* (Philippians 4:13). This is assuming that you are following your plan to live a godly life and will stay committed to that plan through the hard times. Every time you resist the devil he gets weaker and you get stronger. Over time, those attacks will lessen and finally will be gone. You are not attacked in areas where you are strong; only in the weak places.

This approach can be applied to any tempting situation where you are hit in those weaker areas. I am not making this simplistic. At times the battle rages and requires fasting, prayer, and sometimes another person to pray with you. The peace you will experience when planting your victory flag as an overcomer, is amazing. Never underestimate the power that is in you, working to bring you to completion.

"Being confident of this, that he who began a good work in you will carry it on to completion until the day of Christ Jesus." Philippians 1:6

Chapter 13

The Sovereignty of God

*From heaven the LORD looks down and sees all
mankind; from his dwelling place he watches
all who live on earth—he who forms the hearts
of all, who considers everything they do.*

Psalm 33:13-15

Does the teaching we've covered thus far mean
that you have to get your life perfect before
you can live in God's rest? Thankfully, it does not.
Otherwise, none of us could ever appropriate all that
God has promised for abundant life on this earth.
You are always a work in progress. God looks at
your heart. His love for you does not depend upon
your performance. His love is already perfect and

unconditional. He will never love you more than He does right now, no matter what fantastic things you do. Because His love is perfect already. He has infinite patience and compassion.

When He observes your attitudes and efforts, He's like a parent watching his/her child toddle through life's learning challenges, smiling and cheering us on. He is serious about sin, however. His plan, outlined in the guidebook for life (Holy Bible), makes it all very clear. When we choose to ignore His plan or choose direct disobedience, there are consequences, just as when your child disobeys you, there are consequences. The beautiful thing about God's plan is that if people just followed it, not leaving out any aspects of it, life would be so different, so purposeful and peaceful. We just don't do that. We make life all about us, striving and planning and figuring things out, all on our own. Then, when things go awry, we get mad at God and whine and cry. Why doesn't God just do this or that. Well, we were created for Him and life is all about Him. I think if you were the one who created the world, the people and everything in it, you would feel you had the right to make the rules. Your job is to love Him, worship and obey Him. Life is all about Him, not all about you. When you get this, you also get that it's reciprocal and His blessings abound in your life.

Sometimes we're just like the Israelites in the Old Testament, murmuring and complaining, grumbling and mumbling. We feel that we have all the answers for how God should run our lives. Truthfully, we have so little comprehension of the awesomeness of God's mind or His ways.

Someone sent me this email that says a lot. (Sorry, it did not come with the author's name)

Me (in a tizzy) : God, can I ask you something?

GOD: Sure.

Me: Promise you won't get mad?

GOD: I promise.

Me (frustrated): Why did you let so much stuff happen to me today?

GOD: What do you mean?

Me: Well I woke up late,

GOD: Yes

Me: My car took forever to start,

GOD: Okay....

Me (growling): At lunch, they made my sandwich wrong and I had to wait

GOD: Hmmmm..

Me: On the way home, my phone went dead, just as I picked up a call

GOD: All right

Me (loudly): And to top it all off, when I got home, I just wanted to soak my feet in my foot massager and relax, but it wouldn't work. Nothing went right today! Why did you do that?

GOD: Well let me see..... the death angel was at your bed this morning and I had to send one of the other angels to battle him for your life. I let you sleep through that.

Me (humbled): Oh...

GOD: I didn't let your car start because there was a drunk driver on your route that might have hit you if you were on the road

Me (ashamed): ....

GOD: The first person who made your sandwich

today was sick and I didn't want you to catch what they have, I knew you couldn't afford to miss work

Me (embarrassed): Oh.....

GOD: Your phone went dead because the person that was calling was going to give a false witness about what you said on that call, I didn't even let you talk to them so you would be covered

Me (softly): I see God

GOD: Oh and that foot massager, it had a short that was going to throw out all of the power in your house tonight. I didn't think you wanted to be in the dark.

Me: I'm sorry God.

GOD: Don't be sorry, just learn to trust me.........in all things, the good and the bad

Me: I WILL trust you God

GOD: And don't doubt that my plan for your day is always better than your plan

Me: I won't God. And let me just tell you God, thank you for everything today.

GOD: You're welcome child. It was just another

day being your God and I love looking after my children.

Scriptural References: II Samuel 22:31, Proverbs 3:5, Hebrews 2:13

God's love and His sovereignty are awesome. He knows all things, past, present and future. He knew us before we were formed in our mother's womb and already had a plan for us before we were. (Psalm 139) Isn't that enough to warrant our trust? People who are intent on trying to control their own lives are existing in an exercise of futility. They attempt to explain away all the beautiful, supernatural events and blessings God gives and reduce Him to a human form. It can't be done. He is not human and His thoughts and ways are so much higher than ours, we will never be able to explain Him. All we have to do is believe Him and trust Him. He calls it childlike faith. The result of that is total, complete inner peace. I don't know anyone without God who has that. The sad part is, I don't know too many Christians who practice what is in God's Word and live in that realm of peace either. It's a choice. The realization that God created and holds the broader, bigger picture, seeing all things from beginning to end, collides with our little, tiny, insignificant picture of what's happening in our lifetime and we foolishly make an assumption that He is not big enough or good enough to fix what we want fixed. How presumptuous of us and how ridiculous as well.

Yet, in spite of it all, He is ever patient, allowing us to throw infantile tantrums, act out in direct disobedience, or go off in a pout and still loves us deeply, drawing us back into His arms and giving us another chance, and another, and another. His love is extravagant! He sacrificed His only Son so that we could have this unconditional, eternal love showered on us forever. Romans 8:1 says, *"There is now therefore no condemnation for those who are in Christ Jesus."* All we have to do is confess our sins, be truthfully repentant, and turn our eyes back to Him, and all is forgiven. He says it's forgotten in His eyes, as far as the east is from the west. One of my favorite names of Jesus is Redeemer. He truly redeems our crazy mistakes and bad choices. *"He works all things together for good for those who love Him and are called according to His purposes."* (Romans 8:28) What an amazing God we have!

God's Character and Nature

Let's take a little review. We can enter God's rest, living a life of inner peace and security, no matter what is going on around us. The path to that goal requires clearing out some cobwebs that cloud our vision. Some of the barriers we've covered include fear, anxiety, stress, negative thinking, lack of faith or trust in God and attacks from the enemy of our souls.

An important step in tearing down these barriers is to understand the true character and nature of God. I have interspersed many of His attributes throughout these chapters. The truth is that if you base your philosophy of life on what you observe, study from secular writers and teachers, or even some television evangelists, you can be in trouble. I am saddened by so many who hate God and openly despise Christians based on what they observe in the world. It is disheartening for sure to see that many churches and so-called Christians exhibit nothing that Jesus taught us to live. People are people and there are hypocrites in any organization, not just in churches. To base your entire belief system on what carnal Christians have shown you, is tragic. If you read the Bible for yourself, and if you begin to understand the character and nature of God, you will have an entirely different comprehension of the magnificent love of God and all that He has done, and is still doing. If you are one of those people and have chosen to read this for whatever reason, I plead with you to read the Bible for yourself, and ask God to illuminate His motives. Understand that people will always fail, but God never will.

The true church of God is not a building somewhere with a name on it, filled with people who are sinning and pretending they're not. The true church is a group of people who surrendered their lives to the control of Jesus Christ and are daily submitted to following His teachings and being in the center of His will. This means they are feeding the hungry, serving the poor, healing the sick and loving, loving, loving as mandated in the scriptures. None of them are perfect, but they are those with hearts that are sincerely seeking to do the will of the Father. If you are not a believer in Christ, they honestly care about you and your soul. They want to see you in heaven with them for all eternity. And they ask God to soften your heart and see His love. They want you to live in peace and security along with them. They are not judging you, as the world does, but hoping against all odds that you will come to know Christ before it is too late.

Carnal Christians are fooling themselves but fooling no one else, including God. What does this have to do with entering His rest? Everything! God expects us to live holy, godly lives, walking in the Spirit, not the flesh. If we are not convicted of our sin and not daily repenting and re-focusing, we are not living in peace. Show me an unhappy, unfulfilled Christian and I'll show you areas of disobedience to God's word. It goes for me as well as for you.

How could a person live in perfect peace if he is trying to be happy in the world's ways and also in God's ways? There is no way that the two can mesh. Now, if you live in God's ways, then He will show you how to do well living in the world. Jesus brought hard teachings. He said the road to heaven is narrow. When people attempt to divide their hearts into both worlds, they lose---in both. Jesus said that the world will hate you because it hates Him. It's no surprise. But, the world hates Him mostly because it does not know or understand Him. The world is focused on self and all that self can attain. The world is all about satisfying desires of the flesh, and holiness is a joke to those who walk in darkness. The sad truth is that those who mock Jesus' teachings and refuse to accept God's ways, are actually condemning themselves. They never find peace or rest for their souls, though they attempt to find it in myriad ways that never satisfy.

If you are sincere in your quest to abide in peace,

in God's rest, you will make a serious evaluation of your daily attitudes to see how they line up with scripture and then make the decision to lay down some extraneous things that are getting in the way. He will help you! To make an accurate assessment, be sure you have not based your entire theology on a few popular teachers or some relative's opinion. Each one of us stands alone before God at the end of our life. We answer for ourselves only. Telling God that we didn't know any better or that our parents taught us thus and so, won't cut it. Telling him that you followed a great, anointed evangelist won't cut it either. Many of them have teachings which do not line up with scripture. The bottom line is that you are responsible for you. If you submit to the Lord, He will guide you and help you every minute of every day.

Trust in the Lord with all your heart, and lean not on your own understanding. In all your ways acknowledge Him, and He will direct your paths. Prov. 3:5-6.

Chapter 14

Suffering and God's Rest

We rejoice in our sufferings, knowing that suffering produces endurance, and endurance produces character, and character produces hope, and hope does not put us to shame, because God's love has been poured into our hearts through the Holy Spirit who has been given to us. Romans 5:3-5

Suffering is a subject that brings controversy within Christian circles, as well as outside the church. The trendy version is that God doesn't want us to suffer. That sounds so nice. However, that's not what my Bible says. Again, the truth of the Word is only learned through study of the Word. It's not a matter of saying, "God wants you to suffer." That's ridiculous. I have no doubt, after studying the Bible, that God grieves with us over our suffering. He does not delight in it. But, the truth is that God does whatever it takes to accomplish His purposes on the earth. He does whatever is needed to bring people to Him, because His plan is eternal, not temporal. If I need to go through a trial and suffer in order to be refined and used for His purposes, then so be it. He will allow me to suffer. Once again we have to understand that this life is not all about me. It's all about Him. And all about His purpose of conforming us to the image of Christ. You will find example after example of people in Bible history who suffered greatly for the cause of Christ. Today, as well, there are those who suffer daily for their commitment to Him and those who are martyred for their faith. The Bible says their reward is above all the rest.

People who remain in a state of anger because God did not answer a prayer the way they wanted, namely avoiding any suffering, are people who do not understand the bigger picture of life at all. There is a marked lack of trust in God's sovereignty and omniscience and a belief that they know best. What we want and what is best for us are sometimes entirely different issues. How many times have you heard testimonies of those who have survived some horrible tragedy and much later saw and reported the miraculous good that came out of it---usually long lists of good things. However, when we are in the midst of suffering, we rarely can think in those terms. We are basically a selfish people. We want what we want. We definitely do not want to suffer. Even Jesus did not want to suffer when it came down to the last minute before his crucifixion. His human side appeared for a moment. He understands when we feel the same way. He does not condemn us for it.

One of the most difficult scriptures we struggle with is James 1:2-4: "Consider it pure joy, my brothers, whenever you face trials of many kinds, because you know that the testing of your faith develops perseverance. Perseverance must finish its work so that you may be mature and complete, not lacking anything." And don't forget this one: Romans 5:3 "We also rejoice in our sufferings, because we know that suffering produces perseverance, perseverance character, character hope.." And finally, James 1:12 "Blessed is the man who perseveres under trial, because when he has stood the test, he will receive the crown of life that God has promised to those who love Him."

In all these scriptures, we are instructed to have joy

when we are suffering. That is a challenge. However, the promises we have for persevering and considering it all joy are blessings and rewards enjoyed for all eternity. That should be motivating! God is more interested in our character than in our happiness. Some people do not like to hear that. He is molding us and forming us into the likeness of His son, Jesus Christ. We don't always want to be molded. We are rather like spoiled children who always want our way. If He always gave us our way, we would not have any depth of character at all.

I would never presume to try to answer all the "whys" of the ways of God. I do not know why He does what He does. I am not supposed to know. Only He is God. All I am supposed to know is that He created the world, and me, and His plans for me are good. I have to trust that He knows best, even when I have to give up something, someone or some dream I have held onto. Why children die, or why people starve on the streets or why innocent people are hurt is left to the inadequate opinions of our finite minds.

Many situations occur solely because we, the people, have not reached out to care for needs as Jesus taught us to do. We have been poor stewards of our resources, our responsibilities and to our obedience to God's plan. We blame everyone else and God, but usually do not take responsibility for our own part in our world's condition. Yes, we suffer, and our prayer should be that our suffering would always produce top notch fruit. Our prayers should be that when suffering comes, as it does to everyone, that we will persevere and accept whatever God wants us to learn through it. It is the ultimate level of trust. And, it also brings peace to our souls.

Is it really possible to be at peace, in God's rest in the midst of suffering? Yes. If it was not possible, He would not have encouraged us to do it. That's the bottom line. We grow through our trials. Becoming mature is important. When we refuse and stay immature, it reflects everywhere we go, and thus, turns lost hearts even farther from God. That's the real tragedy. An old story you may have heard, still resonates with wisdom:

As Silver Refined

There was a group of women in a Bible study on the book of Malachi. As they were studying chapter three, they came across verse three, which says: "He will sit as a refiner and purifier of silver. "

This verse puzzled the women and they

wondered what this statement meant about the character and nature of God.

One of the women offered to find out the process of refining silver and get back to the group at their next Bible Study. That week, this woman called up a silversmith and made an appointment to watch him at work.

She didn't mention anything about the reason for her interest beyond her curiosity about the process of refining silver. As she watched the silversmith, he held a piece of silver over the fire and let it heat up. He explained that in refining silver, one needed to hold the silver in the middle of the fire where the flames were hottest, so as to burn away all the impurities.

The woman thought about God holding us in such a hot spot --then she thought again about the verse that says, "He sits as a refiner and purifier of silver."

She asked the silversmith if it was true that he had to sit there in front of the fire the whole time the silver was being refined. The man answered that yes, he not only had to sit there holding the silver, but he also had to keep his eyes on the silver the entire time it was in

the fire. If the silver was left a moment too
long in the flames, it would be destroyed.

The woman was silent for a moment. Then
she asked the silversmith, how do you
know when the silver is fully refined?

He smiled at her and answered, "Oh that's
easy -- when I see my image in it."

Author Unknown

The refining fire is indeed hot. We never enjoy it.
I certainly don't. I have been put through the fire
countless times in my life thus far, and I have no
doubt that God isn't finished with me yet. I'd love
to tell you that I always count it all joy when I'm in
the fiery furnace, but that would be a lie. I'm just
like you; I cry, I complain and I ask God to stop the
madness. However, I have seen over the years that I
seem to have what I call a faster turnaround time now
than I used to have. I have learned to get quiet before
the Lord and ask Him to reveal His purposes in my
trials and He usually does, over time. Sometimes I
have to wait until it's passed before I understand the
purpose for it. The apostle Paul said,

"I have learned to be content whatever the

circumstances. I know what it is to be in need, and I know what it is to have plenty. I have learned the secret of being content in any and every situation, whether well fed or hungry, whether living in plenty or in want. I can do everything through Christ who gives me strength."
Philippians 4:11-13

Christ does give us the strength needed for every situation we find ourselves in, if only we give Him the chance to do so.

He came to earth as a human so He would understand our plight. *"We do not have a high priest who is unable to sympathize with our weaknesses, but we have one who has been tempted in every way, just as we are — yet was without sin"* (Hebrews 4:15). Jesus knows what it's like to suffer and to be tempted to give up. He can strengthen us, if we trust him. Trusting Him leads us into His perfect resting place, the shadow of His wings.

Chapter 15

Hebrews 4: Sabbath Rest

"Let us, therefore, make every effort to enter that rest, so that no one will fall by following their example of disobedience." Hebrews 4:11

The Israelites spent 40 years wandering in the desert enroute to the Promised Land; a trip that should have taken about eleven days. They grumbled, complained and refused to follow God's instructions, but He kept giving them more opportunities to get it right. The author of Hebrews cautions:

Therefore, since the promise of entering His rest still stands, let us be careful that none of you be found to have fallen short of it. For we also have had the gospel preached to us, just as they did;

but the message they heard was of no value to them, because those who heard did not combine it with faith. Now we who have believed enter that rest, just as God has said, "So I declared on oath in my anger, 'They shall never enter my rest.'" Hebrews 4:1-3

The entering into His rest in this passage is not a physical rest; it is spiritual. Just as entering physical rest in Canaan demanded faith in God's promise, so salvation—rest is entered only by faith in Jesus Christ. The rest God calls us to enter is not our rest but His rest, which He invites us to share. As we share, we also rest.

Verse 9: There remains then, a Sabbath-rest for the people of God; for anyone who enters God's rest also rests from his own work, just as God did from His.

In Hebrew, the word for rest is "nuach" which goes beyond quietness or peace. It is an all encompassing penetrating sanctuary for the Spirit of God to indwell. The only way to experience that level of resting is to be fully surrendered to Him.

The people I know who are constantly arguing and questioning the Bible and God are also the ones who cannot find peace. It seems to be a quest for answers that appease the human nature instead of realizing that our fleshly needs are always in conflict with God's divine nature. One of my favorite sayings that is posted on my refrigerator is "anything that strengthens the flesh weakens the spirit." It's a reminder that what we want isn't necessarily what's best. God's ways are higher than our ways, and that is one truth that makes His ways so inspiring and motivating! We are always a work in progress and we never run out of fresh truths from His repertoire to move us in a direction of growth.

We have to stop fighting His ways, fabricating good sounding approaches to life that consistently fail and surrender our will to His. Falling forward into His arms of strength and following the plan He laid out thousands of years ago is the only way to navigate life's trials without needing psychiatric help.

Most of our anxiety could be prevented if we simply stopped attempting to prove that we are in control. I am reminded of a Shirley MacLaine movie where she is standing on the beach with the waves rolling in, her arms outstretched toward the sky, calling out, "I am a little god." God Himself was probably shaking His head and chuckling. He could have sent one rolling wave to wash her out to sea in an instant if

He wanted. We don't brazenly state that we are a god, but we certainly behave that way many times, in our efforts to convince others (and ourselves) that we are in control.

Our culture today is so enlightened, so educated, so empowered and so independent, always seeking more of each of those assets, that we begin to believe our own press releases. Any TV talk show or current magazine will inspire one to look within oneself to achieve fulfillment. Sadly, observing people today, we do not see many signs of success for those following that agenda. Celebrities project a facade of happiness, but more times than not, we eventually hear tragic testimonies of their inner turmoil.

The older generations value work. The younger generations value information and technology. Both have been guilty of taking these values to extremes and both lead to emptiness when they become gods of their own.

We physically work, then we rest from our work. We examine our emotions to evaluate the wounds interfering with that aspect of rest. However, our spiritual rest is a deeper level of letting go than merely stopping work or relinquishing sin.

Following God by faith, and not by works or

achievement, is the pathway to His rest. We cannot earn our salvation or eternal life. We enter into His rest by faith, which is the gateway to eternal life. It is a forward movement of trust, walking out our belief in Jesus' death and resurrection. It means we trust so fully in what He did for us that we move into a position of surrender which is demonstrated by obedience. Our obedience moves us forward in confidence because of our understanding of Who He is.

I know many fellow believers who know the scriptures and love God and serve Him, but when hard times come, are devastated and hopeless. Why does this unbelief kick in instead of faith kicking in? The moment a stressed person professes faith, trust and belief, something breaks in the spirit realm and positive change begins. If only we could physically see the spirit realm at times, we would never again voice doubt and unbelief.

In his book, "Holiness, Truth, and the Presence of God," Francis Frangipane stated:

"The turmoil caused by unbelief is brought to rest by faith. The strife rooted in unforgiveness is removed by love. Our fearful thoughts, He arrests through trust; our many questions are answered by His wisdom. Such is the mind which has entered the rest of God."

The Israelites never made it into the Promised Land, His Rest, because they were unable to follow Him, trusting Him with faith that the promise was theirs for the taking. Doubt and unbelief kept them out, just as it keeps us out. Our ability to rest in Him throughout our lives is based on our belief in all that He is, which leads us to total trust and obedience day by day. The Promised Land of His rest is defined in scripture as a place with God where one is secure from all external threats and internal anxieties.

Our final rest is our final entrance into the heavenly home He has prepared for us; our Promised Land: the ultimate rest!! It is the fulfillment of all our works on earth in collaboration with our faith and trust. And when we enter His final rest, scripture says our works will follow us. (Rev. 14:13)

My friend Mary Kay McCauley recently shared with me a testimony of how God expressed His feelings to her about His rest and it's far-reaching implications for the body of Christ:

> "My daughter-in-law experienced a long sixty hour labor and delivery of my first grandson, Samuel. As we eagerly awaited this new little

life, I observed how the midwives worked with the rhythm of her labor. During the contraction, they would encourage her to work and accomplish as much action as possible to move the baby through the birth canal. Then they would rest and pray quietly, ending with worship, reminding her of the promises of God. She received nourishment to regain strength. And then the cycle began again as she worked with the next contraction. The Lord spoke to me during this time and said, "This is how my people will need to function in the last days, living in a divine rhythm of rest and work. This is how they will have endurance to overcome the best and worst of times as they give birth to a new age in the Kingdom."

Today, if you hear his word, believe it, and enter his rest.

Chapter 16

Is it Well with My Soul?

"The LORD bless you and keep you; the LORD make his face shine on you and be gracious to you; the LORD turn his face toward you and give you peace." Numbers 6:24-26

After reading thus far, do you wonder if it is possible to live in God's rest while residing on this earth? Like any challenge, if you try to accomplish every change in one day, it will be too overwhelming. However, taking one day at a time and submitting one issue at a time to your Father, will produce incredible results. The goal is worth every effort of submission that you put forth. One day when you are going through the motions of your life, you will suddenly realize that even though there are trials all around

147

you and chaos abounds, you are feeling at peace. It will be a remarkable, eye-opening experience. You will be operating in the peace that surpasses all understanding and knowing that your God is at the control panel, navigating in perfect order. Can you envision this? I certainly hope so.

Many of us have spent years in church, in Bible studies and other groups hearing the scriptures but not applying them to their full capacity. We sing songs about taking up our crosses and suffering for Jesus' sake and surrendering all. Truthfully, we long to mean it; we try to do those things. But if we are honest, we know in our hearts that we have not really surrendered all. One Sunday morning as our pastor was preaching on taking up our cross, I realized that taking up my cross means laying down everything else. I cannot take up my cross if my arms are full of my plans, goals, dreams and activities. My plans and goals may be good ones to anyone evaluating them, but only God's plans matter.

I have always had many dreams and goals. I spent most of my life working to reach those goals, achieve some level of success and prayed to be sure they lined up with His. When my dreams and goals suddenly seemed to be evaporating before my eyes, I did not take it well. I kept arguing with God about how these plans would benefit His Kingdom; how they would cause me to grow spiritually and minister to others as well. God allowed me to wrestle with that for some time. As I struggled, daily talking to Him about why no progress was happening, I slowly began to see the light. I started to become aware that I was singing 'I surrender all', and 'I lay it all down', etc., but I wasn't really laying down my dreams and plans. I was continuing to fight for them.....because they seemed so good!

One day I asked the Lord why He didn't just tell me specifically how to lay it all down and why I needed to do that. He replied clearly to me that just as I attempt to have my counseling clients discover answers for themselves with my guidance, He also wanted me to discover these answers for myself, with His guidance. Okay. After that, things began to become much clearer. I had a lot to lay down and give up. I won't say it was easy. I grieved the loss of my dreams. I fought depression. At times I wondered if He was angry with me, or disciplining me. I felt like Jacob, wrestling with God. (Genesis 32) After several months, I found that I had a different perspective. He gave me a freedom that is hard to explain. I no longer had to focus on my plans. I only had to go to Him, sit in His presence and take instruction for the day.

He told me He would sustain me with daily manna, as long as I stayed close to Him. I did. And He did. He still does.

Losing your life for His sake is losing in order to gain. You gain immeasurably more than you could attain. In Mark, Chapter 8, we read the story of Peter, providing Jesus with practical plans that he had devised. Like us, Peter knew deep down who Jesus was and God's plan for Him, but he impulsively jumped in to present a better plan. Remember what Jesus did? He turned and said "get thee behind me, Satan!" I would not ever want Jesus to say that to me; would you? Peter was focused on man's plans and his own good ideas. They probably were good ideas, but it doesn't matter, if they are not God's plans.

Borrowing from my pastor's sermon again, we seem to have a mindset that equates the American Dream with the Messiah. They are not anywhere near the same thing. We make plans and follow our heart's desires, chasing after success, material goods, great health and all that to us constitutes the "good life." Then we attempt to force God to put His stamp of approval on it, and bingo, we'll be happy! There is nothing in the Word of God to substantiate that theory. Our job as Christians is to know His Word, seek His will and walk in obedience to that. He doesn't care that much about the American Dream. His priority is a miserable, lost and dying world being born again into His Kingdom and surrendered souls laying down their lives for His sake. As I've said before, it's all about Him; not all about me. Most of us know that if and when we submit to Him, obeying His will and abiding in Him, He does give us the desires of our hearts. (Psalm 37:4) However, the sequence of events is up to God, not me. How He accomplishes things is up to Him, not me. And the beauty of it all is that as we surrender to His will, and as our desires change, we find that we are more peaceful and satisfied than we've ever been before. Only God can do that.

How else can we possibly live in His rest? Only when we are free of the shackles of life that weigh us down, striving to attain whatever we're struggling over. Letting go can mean many things, but mostly it means submitting oneself to a much higher and greater Power who has all the right answers that we do not have and allowing Him to run the show, while we rest in Him. The Psalms often say *"My soul finds rest in God alone." (Psalm 62:5 is one).*

Finding rest in God is a blessing we don't want to miss. He does give us the desires of our heart when we are submitted to Him and obedient. When we are loving and carrying out His desires, instead of dreaming up our own, we move into another dimension, one in which stress and worry dissolve away before our eyes. His dreams become ours and that alignment opens the heavens and showers us with peace. Why do we spend years fighting against that? Because we haven't learned these key truths that change lives and in turn change the world.

In the days to come, it is possible that our nation will be undergoing some difficult and dark days. How will we face each day if we do not have that trust and faith that our God is able to deliver us, protect us, provide for us and sustain us. The truth is, we will not make it without Him. His peace, His wisdom and His daily instruction will be our salvation. Learning to enter His rest now means that when those difficult days come, we will be in shape for the workout to end all tests of endurance. It means that we will rest in knowing that His mercies are new every morning. We will rest in His amazing grace when all around us seems to be in chaos. When our neighbors appear to be falling apart over the economy or the devastation of an earthquake, or war or famine or whatever befalls us, we will be the ones who will be the light bearers, the encouragers, the givers of hope...more importantly, the ones leading them to the One true Giver of hope. We'll be singing "It is well with my soul" and they will be wondering how on earth we could feel that way.

When you board an airliner, you spend a few minutes listening to the stewardess instruct in case of an emergency landing. She coaches parents to apply their oxygen mask first; then place one on their children. You must get a grip on the situation before you minister to another. When you have learned to take your anxieties to the Lord and rest in Him, you will be able to explain the concept to those in despair. They will observe your peace and your strength, walking in the security of who you are in Christ, at rest in His arms.

Entering His rest on a daily basis will lead you into His eternal rest, a heavenly place that never sees a burden, a tear, or any pain whatsoever; only joy forevermore! In reality, we may not ever live totally in His rest until the day He takes us into our eternal home, but the closer we can get, the better! It means that the quality of our lives on this earth is richer and deeper and that is worth so much.

Did you ever hear the story behind the old hymn, "It is Well With My Soul"?

It Is Well With My Soul by Horatio G. Spafford

When peace, like a river, attendeth my way,
When sorrows like sea billows roll;
Whatever my lot, Thou has taught me to say,
It is well, it is well, with my soul.

It is well, with my soul,
It is well, with my soul,
It is well, it is well, with my soul.

Though Satan should buffet, though trials should come,
Let this blest assurance control,
That Christ has regarded my helpless estate,
And hath shed His own blood for my soul.

It is well, with my soul,
It is well, with my soul,
It is well, it is well, with my soul.

This hymn was written by a Chicago lawyer, Horatio G. Spafford, a man who had suffered almost unimaginable personal tragedy. Spafford's only son was killed by scarlet fever at the age of four. A year later, it was fire rather than fever that struck. All his business holdings were wiped out by the great Chicago Fire. Aware of the toll that these disasters had taken on the family, Horatio decided to take his wife and four daughters on a holiday to England. just before they set sail, a last-minute business development forced Horatio to delay. Not wanting to ruin the family holiday, Spafford persuaded his family to go as planned. He would follow on later. With this decided, Anna and her four daughters sailed East to Europe while Spafford returned West to Chicago. Just nine days later, Spafford received a telegram from his wife in Wales. It read: "Saved alone."

On November 2nd 1873, the 'Ville de Havre' had collided with 'The Lochearn', an English vessel. It sank in only 12 minutes, claiming the lives of 226 people. Anna Spafford had stood bravely on the deck, with her daughters Annie, Maggie, Bessie and Tanetta clinging desperately to her. Her last memory had been of her baby being torn violently from her arms by the force of the waters. Anna was only saved from the fate of her daughters by a plank which floated beneath her unconscious body and propped her up. When the survivors of the wreck had been rescued,

Mrs. Spafford's first reaction was one of complete despair. Then she heard a voice speak to her, "You were spared for a purpose." And she immediately recalled the words of a friend, "It's easy to be grateful and good when you have so much, but take care that you are not a fair-weather friend to God." Upon hearing the terrible news, Horatio Spafford boarded the next ship out of New York to join his bereaved wife. Bertha Spafford (the fifth daughter of Horatio and Anna born later) explained that during her father's voyage, the captain of the ship had called him to the bridge. "A careful reckoning has been made", he said, "and I believe we are now passing the place where the de Havre was wrecked. The water is three miles deep." Horatio then returned to his cabin and penned the lyrics of his great hymn.

The words which Spafford wrote that day come from 2 Kings 4:26. They echo the response of the Shunammite woman to the sudden death of her only child. Though we are told "her soul is vexed within her", she still maintains that 'It is well." And Spafford's song reveals a man whose trust in the Lord is as unwavering as hers was. www.biblestudycharts.com

I doubt that I would exhibit faith and trust as unwavering as either of the Spaffords, but that is the rest of God that I long to be able to enter and abide in.

The truth is that it is a choice we make. Years ago, a friend who was attempting to teach her children to make healthy choices, taught them the name of soft drinks was "bad choice." The little ones would run up to her at some event, pointing to the soda pop machine, saying, "Mommy, please can I have a bad choice today?" We want to walk in such peace with God and with ourselves that only the good choices become routine. God will allow us to hold onto the bad choice, the stress, fear and anxiety, but it grieves His heart.

It appears to me that the basic keys to living in God's rest are a clear understanding of God's character and nature, joined with complete trust in Him, walking by faith each and every day. I am committed at this point in my life to entering His rest on a daily basis. It means going through my checklist of bad choices and turning away from them with determination and trust that He will hold my hand and guide me through the rough roads I encounter. I have not achieved perfection in this area by any means, but it gets easier all the time. The rest I find is water to my thirsty soul. Healing and hope abound. I pray the same for you.

Resting Place

Here Oh Lord
Have I prepared a resting place
Here Oh Lord I wait for You alone
-Brian Doerksen

"Now arise, O LORD God, and come to Your resting place, You and the ark of Your might. May Your priests, O LORD God, be clothed with salvation, may Your saints rejoice in Your goodness. -*2 Chronicles 6:41

APPENDIX A

Below are some scriptures regarding our identity as God's children. Pray these verses daily, applying them to your life and you will find a new strength in walking out your identity in Christ.

I am chosen of God, holy and dearly loved. Colossians 3:12

I am a member of a chosen race, a royal priesthood, a holy nation, a people for God's own possession. 1 Peter 2:5

I have been bought with a price; I am not my own; I belong to God.   1 Corinthians 6:19-20

I am one of God's living stones, being built up in Christ as a spiritual house.   1 Peter 2:5

I am God's child. John 1:12

I am a joint heir with Christ, sharing His inheritance with Him. Romans 8:17

I am God's workmanship---His handiwork---born anew in Christ to do His work.
Ephesians 2:10

I am a temple—a dwelling place of God. His Spirit and His life dwells in me.
1 Corinthians 3:16, 6:19

I have been justified---completely forgiven and made righteous. Romans 5:1

I have received the spirit of God into my life that I might know the things freely given to me by God. 1 Corinthians 2:12

Taken from Victory over the Darkness
Dr. Neil Anderson

APPENDIX B

The Full Armor of God

Ephesians 6:10-18 (NIV)

The Armor of God

10 Finally, be strong in the Lord and in his mighty power. 11Put on the full armor of God, so that you can take your stand against the devil's schemes. 12 For our struggle is not against flesh and blood, but against the rulers, against the authorities, against the powers of this dark world and against the spiritual forces of evil in the heavenly realms. 13Therefore put on the full armor of God, so that when the day of evil comes, you may be able to stand your ground, and after you have done everything, to stand. 14 Stand firm then, with the belt of truth buckled around your

waist, with the breastplate of righteousness in place, 15 and with your feet fitted with the readiness that comes from the gospel of peace. 16In addition to all this, take up the shield of faith, with which you can extinguish all the flaming arrows of the evil one. 17 Take the helmet of salvation and the sword of the Spirit, which is the word of God. 18 And pray in the Spirit on all occasions with all kinds of prayers and requests. With this in mind, be alert and always keep on praying for all the Lord's people.

The apostle Paul gives this critical teaching to inform us that we always have a spiritual war actively in process around us. The armor is compared to the Roman soldiers' of Paul's day and each piece is symbolic in reference to our spiritual life. Entire books have been written on this passage, so understand that this small explanation will not do it justice, and dig into a deeper study for yourself.

Our struggle is not against flesh and blood. The unseen forces at work are evil. At times we must be reminded that when an attack from a human comes against us, it is actually the enemy of our souls working through that person. The enemy knows our weakest points and those weaknesses are his targets.

This passage is about each individual's personal need

to stand firm against these attacks. The symbolic clothing reminds us that we are warriors. Our character and our understanding of God's strength at work in and through us produces the victory in each and every battle. It is important to understand the symbolism of each piece of the armor and how it applies to every life as a born again believer. When that is deeply ingrained, we automatically stand firm and see victory.

Elements of the armor   Ephesians 6:10-18 (NIV)

Belt of Truth: Jesus said, "I am the way, the truth and the life; no one comes to the Father except through me" He is the truth. Satan, on the other hand, is known as the father of lies. If we are wearing the belt of truth, it means we have the truth firmly attached to our being and are unwilling to accept the lies of the enemy.

Breastplate of Righteousness: The Roman soldier's breastplate was covering the breast to protect his heart. Arrows flying into that breastplate could not pierce the heart or other vital organs. When we accept Jesus Christ as our Lord and Savior, scripture tells us that we become the righteousness of Christ; in other words, His righteousness abides within us. That righteousness guards our hearts.

Shoes Fitted with the Gospel of Peace: The soldier not only had to protect his feet due to his constant walking miles during battles, he also had to be sure they fit properly. Fitting our feet with the readiness to go share the gospel of Christ with others is becoming a bearer of peace.

Shield of Faith: The shield used by soldiers was large and strong, providing protection from the arrows targeting his body. Satan's fiery darts aimed at us are deflected by our shield of faith.

Faith is believing without any doubt that God's promises to us are trustworthy.

Helmet of Salvation: The helmet covers our head, but it's primary purpose is to protect our minds. When we put on the helmet of salvation, we are declaring our allegiance to Jesus, submitting ourselves to Him as our Savior and Lord. That helmet covers our thoughts, plans, intentions, knowledge and intellect. Salvation in Jesus' terms means our minds cannot be infiltrated by the enemy, unless we take it off and intentionally discard it.

Sword of the Spirit: The sword is the only offensive weapon included in the armor. The sword of the Spirit is the Word of God. When Jesus was tempted by Satan in the desert, he countered every attack with scripture, and walked away victorious. Our weapon against the enemy is God's Word. Praying God's Word sends the enemy and his minions packing.

Prayer: Pray in the Spirit on all occasions with all kinds of prayers and requests. Prayer is the covering that initializes the Spirit realm. Prayer is the key to victory. Prayer is our communion with our Father, and leads us into His perfect will for our lives. Prayer is our greatest weapon against the enemy. Prayer is our connection to the Father's heart.

FULL ARMOR OF GOD

Helmet of
Salvation

Breastplate of
Righteousness

Sword of The
Spirit

Belt of
Truth

Shield
of Faith

PRAYER

Shoes of The
Gospel of Peace

NOTES

Made in the USA
Middletown, DE
29 August 2022